Gospel Church
Government

Grace
Publications

GRACE PUBLICATIONS TRUST
62 Bride Street
London N7 8AZ
www.gracepublications.co.uk

First published in Great Britain by Grace Publications Trust 2012.
This edition 2024.

A record for this book is available from the British Library.

Cover design by Pete Barnsley (CreativeHoot.com)

ISBN Paperback: 978-1-912154-91-3
        Ebook: 978-1-912154-92-0

Printed and bound in UK by Ashford Colour Press

Gospel Church Government

An updated and shortened version of *'The True Nature of a Gospel Church and Its Government'* by John Owen, first published in 1689.

The original is available in John Owen, *Collected Works*, Volume 16 (Banner of Truth, 1968).

Simplified and abridged by
Jeffrey T. Riddle

Grace
Publications

Contents

Introduction

While John Owen has long been popular among Reformed Christians and many of his works have been well known, his little book on local church theology has been sadly neglected. Owen's writings are notoriously cumbersome, and Jeff Riddle has done the church a tremendous service with his careful adaptation of Owen's rather more complicated prose. The substance of Owen's thought is here clearly presented in a more accessible form of English. But what is this book on Gospel Church Government?

The *True Nature of a Gospel Church* is a fantastic manual on both local church order and the theology of pastoral ministry. There are a number of key emphases in this lesser-known work. Owen's discussion on what the church is provides a helpful reminder of the importance of beginning with Scripture whenever we discuss questions about the local church. His emphasis on the biblical and historical precedent for congregationalism will be an encouragement to many a Congregational and Baptist pastor at least, and potentially many others as well. Owen's description of the pastoral office is one of my favourite Puritan descriptions of what it means to be a shepherd of Christ's sheep. The discussion on church discipline is also timely as churches wrestle with not only what following Christ looks like but also how to deal with members who fall into unrepentant sin. The end of the work reminds independent churches that working together has long been a key part of independent church life.

Not all readers will agree with all of what Owen writes. For example, his distinction between the pastor and teaching elders is somewhat unique to his own time (at least in congregational polity), and indeed resembles Presbyterianism more than current day forms of Congregationalism. But readers new to Owen will find much to make them think about the New Testament's emphasis on the local church, and readers familiar with Owen's depth of theology and insight into the Christian life will be pleased to see Owen's thoughts on local church ministry receive new attention.

Aaron Prelock

Pastor and PhD (VID University Stavanger, Norway) in
Owen's practical theology

Preface

John Owen (1616-1683) was a man whose conscience was captive to the Word of God. This 'prince of the English divines' is perhaps best known for his weighty doctrinal treatises like *The Death of Death in the Death of Christ* and his rich devotional writings like *Communion with God*. One should not overlook, however, his significant contributions to the doctrine of the church. Sinclair Ferguson has noted that for Owen and the Puritans 'ecclesiology was a vitally important aspect of the Christian life' (*John Owen on the Christian Life*, Banner of Truth, 1987, p. 154).

As a young minister Owen staunchly defended the Presbyterian form of church government in *The Duty of Pastor and People Distinguished* (1643). After reading John Cotton's *The Keys of the Kingdom* (1644), however, Owen's convictions began to shift. He soon embraced the congregational form of church government. Owen then became a leader among congregational and independent ministers in England and was one of the principal authors of *The Savoy Declaration* (1658). He clearly had a significant influence on the early Particular Baptists who drew from both *The Westminster Confession of Faith* and *The Savoy Declaration* in framing the influential *Second London Baptist Confession of Faith* (1689).

According to a preface to *The True Nature of a Gospel Church and Its Government* attributed to Isaac Chauncey, Owen wrote this work to respond to 'most vigorous assaults made upon separate and congregational churches.' This preface adds that Owen 'lived to finish it under his great bodily infirmities, whereby he saw himself hastening to the end of his race'. Indeed, he was apparently able to complete the work and correct the copy before his death in 1683, though it was not published until 1689. In this book, Owen presents his mature reflections on the biblical doctrine of the church. This includes a high view, under Christ, both of the role of the congregation in the government of a local church body and of the role of her officers (pastors, teachers, ruling elders, and deacons). Owen also addresses a biblical understanding of church discipline, while attempting to correct abuses and offer practical counsel. Finally, he stresses the importance of local churches sharing in 'communion' (fellowship) with other like-minded gospel churches.

It has been my pleasure to contribute to this simplification and abridgement of Owen's classic work under the new title *Gospel Church Government*. Those who compare this volume closely with Owen's original work will find that I have sometimes significantly abridged his arguments. In some places I have also combined several of his original points. This means that the presentation or numbering of points in this volume do not always correspond to that found in the original.

Most notably, those who make this comparison will notice that Owen's original consisted of eleven chapters, while this volume has only ten chapters. This is due to the fact that this volume combines Owen's original chapter seven on the Ruling Elder and chapter eight on The Nature of Ruling into a single chapter under the title 'The office of ruling elder'. Most importantly, however, I have tried to maintain the spirit, and often even the letter, of Owen's original wording, while also conveying the essence of his thought in a much simpler and more accessible form for modern readers. It is my hope that many who read this volume might even be encouraged to take up and read Owen's original work with increased understanding. My prayer is that the timeless substance of this book will prove valuable to any who desire to see Christ's church more nearly conformed to the scriptural pattern.

Jeffrey T. Riddle
Pastor, Christ Reformed Baptist Church
Louisa, Virginia, USA.

Chapter 1

Who belongs to a church?

Let us first consider what people rightly belong to the church. What sort of people does the Lord Jesus Christ make citizens of his kingdom? Any good society requires good citizens. The Bible calls the people who become part of God's kingdom (the church) *saints*. They are his holy ones. They are separated from the world. It should be clear that those living in open sin and who are ignorant of the gospel do not belong in church membership. We should consider four important factors:

1. Christ requires much of those who become members of his church. If much is expected of citizens in earthly kingdoms, how much more is expected of citizens in Christ's kingdom?

2. Every member of Christ's church must experience regeneration. He must be born again.

3. Every believer should be baptised. Baptism is the outward symbol or sign of what has happened inwardly.

4. God alone is the judge of the real state of the souls of men. The church can only be the judge of the outward fruits and no more.

How do we form right judgments?

The following points will help us form right judgments about who can be part of a gospel church:

1. No one can become a member of the church who lives in open and habitual sin. We must withdraw fellowship from those who claim to be Christians but live in that way. To compose churches of habitual sinners is not to erect temples to Christ but chapels to the devil.

2. No one can become a member of the church who has committed a scandalous sin and refuses to repent.

3. Church members of today should match the description of the members of gospel churches in the Bible. If they do not, the church will not be built up but destroyed. The church members of old were called saints. They were living stones in the house of God. They were justified and sanctified. They were separated from the world. If such requirements are ignored or denied today, it only shows how far the Christian religion has fallen.

4. Church members must openly profess faith in Christ. They must submit themselves to his authority. They must be ready to obey all his commands (see Rom. 10:10;

2 Cor. 8:5; 9:13; Mt. 10:32-33; Lk. 9:26; 2 Tim. 2:12; Rom. 15:9; Jn. 12:42; 1 Jn. 4:2,3,15).

What is required of church members?

Church members must have a genuine profession of faith. Here are the requirements of such a profession:

1. It requires a right understanding of the gospel. This includes a right understanding of who Christ is and what he came to do. The risen Christ gave his apostles a commission to teach and to preach the gospel. If a person is ignorant of the fundamental doctrines of the gospel, he should not be admitted into church membership. If he is, Christ's church will be defiled.

2. It requires submission to the authority of Christ in the church (Mt. 28:18-20; 2 Cor. 8:5). The first sign of this submission is when a believer is baptised in the name of Christ.

3. It requires self-denial and cross-bearing. Our Saviour taught this to his disciples (see Mt. 10:37-39; Mk. 8:34,38; Lk. 9:23). It is a shame that we do not teach this more clearly in our day. It is often thought that it is easy to become a Christian or that it will cost us nothing. The gospel, however, gives us another account. It warns of hostility, hatred, sufferings, and often even death itself for believers. A person should consider this before making a commitment to Christ. This used to be taught in the early church. In particular, faithful ministers of the

gospel need always to be prepared for suffering. It is not consistent with the gospel to escape sufferings by sinful compromise.

4. It requires conviction and confession of sin, and a trust in the way of deliverance by Jesus Christ.

5. It requires the steady performance of all spiritual duties. This includes the public and private worship of God as well as personal ministry to others.

6. It requires a life free from sin that is scandalous in the eyes of the world and the church of God (1 Cor. 10:32; Phil. 1:10).

Who should be excluded from church membership?

The following people should not be admitted to church membership: (1) those who do not understand the gospel; (2) those who persecute Christians; (3) those who worship and serve idols; (4) those living in scandal; and (5) those who will not submit to the commands of Christ in the gospel.

We cannot improve on the example of the early church. They preached the gospel to all they could. They rejoiced that multitudes came to hear the Word. However, if anyone attempted to join with them, they were diligent in examination and instruction. They asked serious questions about a person's conversion before admitting him into membership. They knew that admitting unqualified people into church membership ruins all the beauty, order and discipline of the church.

Members of the visible church are properly called 'saints', 'the called' and 'the sanctified'. These were the titles used in the New Testament church and we should follow this same pattern. We can tell if those who claim to be Christians are hypocrites by listening to their words but also by looking at what they do, which will reveal what they really think.

Scripture never teaches that Christ received unqualified people into his church. No one can deny that members of the church should be holy. To claim to belong to the church while living in sin is a denial of the gospel and sinful rebellion against the rule of Christ.

What can we learn from church history?

The early church faced persecution from outside, but it still preserved discipline inside. We need to imitate those early churches. We should not be like the churches during the times of the 'Christian' emperors. At this time, all things began to rush into apostasy. When the Roman emperors embraced Christianity the outward peace of the church was secured, but the care and diligence of the churches in admitting members was largely lost. The rulers of the church began to think that glory consisted in *numbers*. They wanted to increase their own power and wealth. In a short time, the population of whole cities and provinces were admitted into churches. This corrupted the church in doctrine, worship, order and rule. It ended in the great apostasy. The church became confused with the state and the result was the ruin of the church in all its order and beauty.

Even in the Protestant Reformation the issue of church membership was not clearly addressed. The great Reformers worked principally against the false doctrine and false worship of Rome. They believed that false doctrine and false worship had filled the people with darkness and they were correct as far as they went. However, the reformation of the church in its membership was not attempted at that time. It was only when Calvin came to Geneva that the purity of the church began to be addressed. In most other places, the churches continued largely as they were under the old papal system.

A progressive reformation was God's holy and wise plan. This served for the good of the church. If the Reformers had started with church membership, their efforts to reform doctrine and worship would have slowed down. In our day, the process of reformation is continuing. Churches are still conforming themselves to the New Testament pattern.

The central message of this book is that church membership should be biblical. Christ is the head of the church, and we are his body (1 Cor. 12:27; Eph. 2:22; 1 Cor. 3:16-17; 2 Cor. 8:5). Sadly, many church members are not what they ought to be. Many are hypocrites, and we must make honest judgments.

How do I find a good church?

We must also ask how a Christian can find a good church. What if he belongs to a church that does not have a pure membership? What if his church does not even care about biblical standards for church membership? Here are my answers:

1. A Christian should only stay in a church if he is being edified. Does the church build up the believer in the faith? No man is obliged to remain in the fellowship of a church if he is not being edified.

2. A Christian should leave a corrupt church. It is corrupt if the lives of its members dishonour the gospel. It is corrupt if it fails to represent the holiness of Christ and his doctrine. It is also corrupt if it does not, cannot, or will not reform itself. In such cases, it is the duty of any Christian to withdraw from the membership of that church. He should do this as peacefully as possible. He must then find a true church.

To withdraw offers a testimony against the weakness of such churches. They bring dishonour to the gospel. All believers must first be the loyal subjects of their Lord and King. It is as justified to withdraw from a church over the issue of membership as it is to withdraw over doctrine or worship. It is better for believers to depart from corrupt churches than to stay to the ruin of their own souls.

How should the church care for those who cannot be received into full membership?

This category includes children who come from Christian homes but who are not yet believers. It also includes servants (employees) or other household members who might attend church with a Christian family, but who do not know the Lord. I believe that the church and its officers should seek to take these under its spiritual care. It is, in fact, a great evil if they do not. The duty of the church to these people consists in prayer for them, instructing them according to their ability, advising their parents (in the case of children), visiting them in their families, encouraging or warning them, and preparing them, if converted, for joining the church. They are excluded, however, from participation in the special privileges of the church.

Churches need to be careful not to neglect this duty. Neglect arises from factors such as: (1) ignorance of this duty; (2) not enough officers and teachers in many churches; (3) the lack of a sense of duty in parents and masters; and (4) failure properly to value the great privilege of having such people under the church's care.

Churches need to have enough officers to attend to all their duties. Families must be dedicated to God. Where there are godly officers and strong families, you will find church-order, usefulness and beauty.

What is the special duty of a church in admitting members during a time of great persecution?

In the days of the apostles and the early church they were careful not to admit members who might betray them. However, they did not allow concern for their own safety to keep them from admitting genuine Christians. This is the rule in which we should walk. In times of persecution, the church is obliged to receive sincere converts into its care and fellowship. They prove their sincerity if they profess faith in the truth of the gospel and are ready to suffer for it. They prove their sincerity if they flee from scandalous sins and submit to the rule of Christ in the church. If a church refuses to admit them, these new converts might be cast off into superstition and idolatry. In the end, how will a church be able to explain such a refusal to the great Pastor of the whole flock?

Chapter 2
How is a church formed?

Believers become a church through a solemn agreement. They agree to perform the duties that Christ has given to his disciples in the churches. They also agree to exercise the power entrusted to them by the rule of the Word. For the most part, churches today do not understand this. They just follow traditions. Few think that any act or duty is required of them to become part of a church or to remain in one. To understand what a church is truly supposed to be we must understand how it began.

New Testament churches, planted or gathered by the apostles, were particular churches. Each of these churches consisted of many members. If a person was a member of one local church, he was not a member of another. The saints of the church at Corinth were not members of the church at Philippi. How did believers in one place become a church that was distinct from others? The Scriptures generally affirm that in one local church they gave themselves up to the Lord and to the apostles (2 Cor. 8:5). Then, other believers were added to this church (Acts 2:47). It is the will and command of our

Lord that all his disciples should be joined in such societies. All disciples must learn to obey Christ's commands (Mt. 28:19-20).

A church can be formed only by the willing consent of its members. There are various requirements for membership. Each person must profess faith in the Lord. Each person must be baptised. Each person must live in the same area where the church will meet. They must all be willing to listen to the preaching and teaching of the Word in the same place. Yet a group of people may do these things and still not form a particular church.

A particular church also requires the proper exercise of discipline and rule. A church is entrusted with power and privileges. It creates a new relationship among the members who belong to it, just as marriage changes the relationship between the husband and wife. While this can only come about by joint consent, the only one who can truly form a church is the Lord Jesus Christ.

Every human society requires that its members consent to it laws and observe them. Christ, by his own authority, has appointed and instituted churches. He has granted powers and privileges to churches. He requires and commands all his disciples to join themselves to churches. This joining is a voluntary act of faithful obedience to the authority of Christ.

To join a church therefore requires a covenant commitment. In the Bible God often called upon men to make covenants. In a covenant, a person makes a commitment to fulfil a duty. God offers special promises for covenant obedience. A church membership covenant is not the covenant of grace, but it is a gospel duty in the covenant of grace. The more we express our commitment to the local church the more we glorify Christ. We receive great encouragement in living the Christian life through the local church.

The Lord Christ also instituted and appointed officers, rulers, or leaders in his church. Their task is to help members grow in faithfulness. This also requires consent. Believers must submit to the pastoral authority of the church officers within the church. Paul explained that the Macedonian believers had given themselves to the Lord and then 'to us by the will of God' (2 Cor. 8:5).

In the Old Testament, God made a covenant with Abraham and his seed. The people made a covenant with God to do all he commanded. By this they became a church. The covenant of grace still continues for the true seed of Abraham (Acts 2:38-39). It is now transferred to gospel worshippers. Those called by the gospel enter a new church where the duties are spiritual and easy. It is, however, still established by a covenant and mutual consent.

Chapter 3
Who rules the church?

We have discussed who should belong to a church. We have also discussed how a church is formed. Our subject now is the power or authority of the church. We can define the rule of the church as the exercise of the power or authority which Jesus Christ has given to the church so that it can be built up (edified). This power is in the church itself, but it still remains Christ's power. All authority in and over the church is given to Christ alone. His power alone is over the souls and consciences of men.

Edification

Jesus Christ grants power and authority to the church only for a ministry of edification. Men often selfishly abuse authority. They use their authority to gain personal wealth and power. The Lord forbids this kind of abuse of power (cf. Lk. 12:25-26; Mt. 20:25-28). Church authority is not like worldly and civil authority. Christ will not tolerate 'lordly power' in his church.

The rule of the church is only to apply the commands and will of Christ to the souls of men.

The nature of the church is destroyed if human authority of any kind is introduced. It makes the church a kingdom of this world. The church is the house of Christ. It is his family. It is his kingdom. To introduce human authority into the church is to invade his dominion. What father would allow any authority to be exercised in his family but his own? What earthly prince would allow such an intrusion into his dominion? The power of rule in the church, then, is nothing but yielding obedience to the commands of Christ. The rulers of the church must understand that they are limited to the use of ministerial power only. They are to use this authority to edify the church, and they are forbidden to use worldly power. The rule of the church is to be spiritual not carnal. It does not use the laws of men but spiritual means for spiritual ends only. Those loyal to Christ will always seek to have his commands rule the church.

Christ's power in the church

How does the power and authority of Christ function in the church?

1. *The Lord Jesus Christ gave extraordinary power to the apostles*. The apostles received this authority even before gospel churches were formed. When churches were gathered under their ministry, even greater authority was given to them (Acts 1:14-15; 6:1-4; 1 Cor. 12:28; Eph. 4:11-15).

2. *This extraordinary power has now ceased in the church.* The office of apostle required: (1) a personal call from Christ himself; (2) a commission to evangelise all nations and to serve all churches; (3) an authority in all churches; (4) extraordinary gifts (infallible teaching, working of miracles, speaking in tongues, etc.). With the passing of the apostolic age, this office and power ceased absolutely. For anyone to pretend to be the successors of the apostles is to plead that Christ has directly called him to this office. That is utter folly.

3. *Christ has not appointed anyone to be his vicar and to distribute authority to others.* Christ exercises his authority in the church by his Word and Spirit. This will continue until the end of the ages. Sober Christians reject the claims of the pope of Rome to have any special authority.

4. *Church officers are not like worldly lords, but they help the saints to grow in Christ.* (See 1 Cor. 2:3; 3:21-23; 2 Cor. 1:24; Eph. 4:11-15; 1 Pet. 5:1-2.) The church is the spouse of Christ, the Lamb's wife. She is due his protection. All officers are her servants for Christ's sake. Though some have stewardship over their fellow servants, they do not rule his spouse by their own will.

5. *Church power is committed to the whole church by Christ.* Those called to serve as officers in the church receive their authority from Christ by his Word and Spirit through the ministry of the church.

Christ's distribution of power

How does Christ distribute power to those in the church?

1. Every believer has power given to him when he becomes a son of God (Jn. 1:12). He has a right to the privileges, advantages and duties of being part of the church, the family of God. This is the foundation of all church power. The Christian's rights are granted to him by his adoption.

2. Wherever there are two or three of these believers (the smallest number), they have the right or power to meet together in the name of Christ for mutual edification. Christ promised to be present among them (Mt. 18:19-20). They have the right to exhort, instruct and admonish one another. They have the right to pray together.

3. When their numbers increase, they have the right to make a joint solemn confession of their faith, especially concerning the person and work of Christ (Mt. 16:16-18). They also may give themselves up to him and to one another in a holy agreement or covenant. In this covenant they agree to do and observe all the things Christ has commanded. When these believers become a church, they immediately have the power to do all the things that Christ commands to be done by his church. This is the basic church to which Christ grants power. It is the place where his ordinances are obeyed in worship. It is the tabernacle in which he dwells. Since the extraordinary offices have ceased, there is no other possible way of forming a church.

4. The church is not yet complete, however, until it has proper officers. The Lord has ordained offices and appointed officers in order to establish the church (Eph. 4:11-15). Church authority is granted to the officers. Christ grants to the church the right and power to call, choose, appoint and set apart people for the offices appointed by him.

The appointment of officers

How does the Lord appoint officers in the church? How does the church recognise these officers? Here are four points to consider:

1. Christ has instituted and appointed the offices and granted them to the church for its edification. No church has the power to appoint any office or officer that Christ has not appointed. Those not appointed by Christ have no authority. All authority of church officers proceeds from the authority of Christ.

2. Wherever Christ calls a church, he acts as head and king over it to supply people with the gifts and abilities needed to serve as officers in that church. Every church office requires those with special abilities and qualifications to fill it. Only Christ can grant these abilities to officers. In their own power, men can no more create officers than they can create an office in the church (cf. Eph. 4:11-15; 1 Cor. 12:4-10 ff.; Rom. 12:6-8). A man may go through the outward process to be appointed to an office, but if he

does not have these special God-given gifts, he is not a true officer in Christ's church.

3. There should be an orderly process for gifted and qualified people to be admitted to their offices. Churches can make reasonable judgments about the process for appointing officers, but a person is only truly made an officer by the appointment of Christ.

4. Christ commands the whole church to submit to the authority of these officers as they fill their office. The officers do not have unlimited power. They are not to act in a 'lordly' manner. They have power only as they rightly fill their office. They are not officers or ministers of men, or of churches, but of Christ himself.

The work or duty of the church is to obey the commands of Christ. The church has a double duty. First, it must call or choose officers. Second, it must voluntarily act with them and submit to them in all their duties of rule.

The special wisdom of officers

A special wisdom and understanding is needed in order to exercise government in the church in the way Christ has appointed. This wisdom is a spiritual gift (1 Cor. 12:8). It enables the officers and the church to apply the rules and laws of Christ for the edification of the church and all its members. The officers receive this wisdom by (1) fervent prayer for it (Jas. 1:5); (2) diligent study of the Scriptures (Ezra 7:10; 2 Tim. 2:1,15); (3) humble waiting on God (Ezek. 43:11); (4) careful exercise of the skill which they have received; and (5) a continual sense of the account which must be given for the responsibility of ruling in the house of God (Heb. 13:17). How much has this wisdom in church government been neglected and even despised in the world!

Two things follow from this:

1. This wisdom is not promised to all the members of the church in general. All are not required to seek it. This is why the obedience of the people to their rulers is so important. Wisdom for rule is specially granted to them. Their duty is to seek after it in a special manner. Therefore, those who seek to advance their own wisdom and understanding against the wisdom of the officers of the church are proud and disorderly.

2. The officers should seek to gain and increase in wisdom. They should give clear and constant evidence of this, so that the church may safely submit to their rule.

Chapter 4

The officers of the church

Order in the church comes from Christ who gives it power. Christ organises a church by placing officers in it. The officers then exercise the authority of Christ in the church. Not all officers, however, are called to rule. There are two major kinds of officers in the church, elders (also called presbyters, overseers or bishops) and deacons (Phil. 1:1). Deacons are explained in Chapter 8. There are two kinds of elder: (1) Some have the authority to teach and administer the sacraments. They also have the authority to rule. (2) Some only have the authority to rule.

Bishops and elders are the same

The Bible teaches that in the early church there were only particular, local, congregations. We therefore reject the idea of bishops who have authority over multiple churches (the episcopal system). That system has led to ambition and scandal in the past. Men should consider how serious it is to be responsible to care for souls. This would curb the desire to enlarge their territory.

In the New Testament, the bishop (overseer) and the presbyter (elder) were the same person. They held the same office and served the same function, with no distinctions in order or degree:

1. Consider the apostle's description of the qualifications for presbyters or elders in Titus 1:5-9. He makes reference here to both the 'bishop' and the 'elder' (vv. 5,7). They are the same person and the same office.

2. Consider Philippians 1:1. The letter is addressed to all the saints at Philippi, with the 'bishops and deacons'. In this one church at Philippi, there were several bishops. There was not one bishop over the elders in many churches!

3. Consider Paul's address to the elders of the church at Ephesus. Again, the titles 'elder' and 'bishop' are used of the same people (Acts 20:17,28). They had the same office, the same function, the same duties, and the same names.

4. Consider Peter's words in 1 Peter 5:1-3. He writes to the 'elders' of the church, urging them to 'feed the flock'. This also means 'to take oversight' or to serve in the office of a bishop over it. They were to do this not as 'lords' but as examples of humility, obedience and holiness to the whole flock. The ones called upon to feed and oversee the flock are bishops. They must give an account to Jesus. They have no other bishop over them. Peter calls these men elders. So, we see again that elders and bishops are

the same. These are also the leaders that the members of the church were urged to obey in Hebrews 13:17. They must give an account of the souls under their care.

5. The witnesses all agree. The Bible teaches that bishops and elders are in every way the same. There is no inequality among them. No one can deny this.

When a church grows to the point that it has many elders, it is nevertheless orderly for one of them to take a leading role in guiding and directing the church. He might be the first one converted or the first ordained. He might be appointed to this role due to his age or his gifts and abilities. He might serve in this role for a season and then have another take his place. This can be decided by the general rules of reason and order for the church's edification.

A special role for one elder among the elders

I will never oppose the practice of one elder playing a leading role. My desire, however, is to stress the fact that particular churches require many elders. This includes both teaching and ruling elders. This helps the teaching and government of the church. It provides order in public assemblies. It best represents the authority Christ has given to the church officers. It helps with teaching members in small gatherings. It helps in all the other aspects of building up the body. It helps in watching, inspecting, warning, admonishing, exhorting and the like. The elders can then choose one among them, with the church's consent, for a special role. This is not a new order or a new office. He does not have a new degree of authority over his fellow elders. He simply serves in a special way. The Scriptures do not teach differences in equality or authority among the same sort of church officers. This is true of both extraordinary and ordinary officers. The apostles were all equal. So too were the evangelists, the elders or bishops, and the deacons. The Bible no more knows of the office of an archbishop or an archdeacon than it does of an archapostle, an archevangelist, or an archprophet! Nevertheless, it is also clear that in all their assemblies one presided in a special manner. Among the apostles in the early days, it was Peter.

The role of the congregation

A church may get so large that it might be difficult for everyone to meet in one place. Still, the witness of the early church is that in serious matters the whole church came together in one place for consultation. We see this in the two great churches of Antioch and Jerusalem in Acts 15. Paul and Barnabas were sent to Jerusalem by the 'brethren' or church at Antioch (vv. 1-3). In Jerusalem, they were received by 'the church', along with 'the apostles and elders' (v. 4). When the apostles and elders assembled, the whole 'multitude' of the church was there (vv. 6,12). They were not mute spectators. They took part in the debate and in the decision making (vv. 22-23). When Paul and Barnabas returned to Antioch, the 'multitude' came together to hear the letter (vv. 23,30). If this pattern is not followed the primitive church order is overthrown!

The office of pastor

The first officer or elder of the church is the *pastor*. A pastor is an elder who feeds and rules the flock (1 Pet. 5:2). He is its teacher and its bishop. The name of *pastor* or *shepherd* is symbolic. The church is called a flock. God calls himself the shepherd of the flock and sent Christ to be 'the good shepherd' and the prince of shepherds. Some who try to take on this office are really 'hirelings' and 'wolves'. People like that devour and destroy the flock (Acts 20:18-19; 1 Pet. 5:2-4; Song 1:7; Jer. 13:17; 23:2; Ezek. 34:3; Gen. 49:24; Ps. 23:1; 80:1; Jn. 10:11 14-16; Heb. 13:20; 1 Pet. 2:25; 5:4). In contrast, the very title *shepherd* implies love, care, tenderness and watchfulness. This is evident in all the duties of leading, preserving, feeding and defending the flock. It is seen in his care for the sheep and the lambs, the strong and the weak, the well and the sick. He is accountable to the Chief Shepherd. The Holy Spirit gave this name to the principal ministers of the church (Eph. 4:11). Under that name, they were promised to the church of old (Jer. 3:15). The work of these pastors is to feed the flock committed to their charge (Acts 20:28; 1 Pet. 5:2). This is a constant requirement.

Pastoral feeding has two parts: (1) teaching or instruction; and (2) rule or discipline. All of the shepherd's work of 'feeding' is included under these two headings (1 Chr. 11:2; 17:6; Jer. 23:2; Mich. 5:4; 7:14; Zech. 11:7; Acts 20:28; Jn. 21:15-17; 1 Pet. 5:2, etc.). Thus, the pastor is the bishop, the elder, the teacher of the church. Pastors are both teachers and rulers. A pastor cannot feed only by teaching. He cannot feed only by ruling. He must do both!

The qualifications of a pastor

What sort of man should be called to the office of pastor? Our great example and pattern is the Lord Jesus himself. The Lord Jesus is the good shepherd. He is the Shepherd and Bishop of our souls. He is the Chief Shepherd. He has provided the model and example for all who are called to this office under him. Here are five Christ-like qualities a pastor is to have:

1. *He must have gifts and abilities given by the Holy Spirit.* Spiritual anointing is required in all who are called to be pastors (Eph. 4:7). A pastor must have spiritual abilities to build up the church. This includes prayer and preaching. The outward call alone cannot make a man an evangelical pastor. No man should be called to this office unless he has spiritual gifts of knowledge, wisdom and understanding. He must also be gifted in prayer and preaching.

2. *He must show compassion and love to the flock.* This was seen in the 'great Shepherd of the sheep'. He lay down his life for them. Here is the example that is continually before pastors. They must have love for the souls of men. If they do not have this love, they may be wolves, hirelings, or thieves, but they are not shepherds.

3. *He must be continually watchful over the whole flock.* The great Shepherd watches over his flock to keep, preserve, feed, lead, cherish, purify and cleanse it. He presents it unspotted to God. He never sleeps. He waters his vineyard every moment. He keeps it night and day. He allows none

to be hurt. He loses nothing committed to him. For the pastor this includes: (1) constant prayer for the flock; (2) diligence in declaring the Word, wisely addressing the needs of the flock; (3) personal admonition, exhortation, comfort and instruction as needed; (4) doing all with the aims of protecting the flock from evil and presenting them without blame to Christ at the great day.

4. *He must have zeal for the glory of God.* This was seen in the whole ministry of the great Shepherd. It was always in his holy soul. He was consumed with zeal for the house of God (Jn. 2:17). Pastors must have this zeal. The lack of it has filled the world with a dead, faithless and fruitless ministry.

5. *He must be set apart.* Christ was 'holy, harmless, undefiled, separate from sinners'. Pastors must be conformed to Christ. They must stand out above others in this quality.

Why do we need pastors?

Some deny that this office is to continue and that there are special duties, including the administration of the sacraments, given to these officers. They maintain that people who have not been called or set apart to this office may do this work as long as the church gives them permission. There have been many disputes about this, so I will briefly explain why we need pastors:

1. *Christ himself created this office.* He gave it, appointed it, and erected it in the church by his own sovereign power and authority (Eph. 4:11-12; 1 Cor. 12:28). As he gave, appointed and ordained the extraordinary office of apostle, so he ordained, appointed and gave the ordinary office of pastor and teacher. They both have divine origins.

2. *He appointed this office to continue.* It is to abide until the consummation of all things (Eph. 4:13; Mt. 28:19-20). Through his apostles, he ordered that pastors, elders and bishops be called and ordained to care for all the churches (Acts 14:22-23; 20:28; 1 Tim. 3:1-7; Tit. 1:5-9).

3. *He gave this office responsibility for the entire order, rule and edification of his church.* He did this in his name and by his authority (Acts 20:28; Col. 4:17; 1 Tim. 3:15; 1 Pet. 5:1-4; Rev. 2:1-5; etc.). We need this office because Christ commanded it and because it is the principal ordinary means given by Christ for the good of the church. Certainly, he can feed his church in the wilderness without means, but when this office is neglected, disorder, confusion and destruction usually follow. Without pastors there is no feeding or edification.

4. *The Lord Christ commands the church to obey those who hold and exercise this office.* These commands would be unnecessary if the office did not continue. The church loses much in grace and privilege if it ignores these commands (see 1 Tim. 5:17; Heb. 13:7,17).

5. *This office holds power and authority that no one can take to himself.* All power and authority, in things spiritual or temporal, must come from God. To take an office improperly disturbs the natural, divine and civil order.

6. *Christ has appointed a continuing rule for calling men to this office.* If there is no office and no call to it, then this rule is given in vain. There is no greater affront to the authority of Christ than to neglect or oppose the rules he has given.

7. *Those who undertake this office will be held accountable.* The preservation of the whole flock, the ministry itself, and the gospel are committed to pastors (Col. 4:17; 1 Tim. 6:20; 2 Tim. 2:2,16,23; Acts 20:28; 1 Pet. 5:1-4; Heb. 13:17). It is both wicked and foolish for a man to take on a responsibility that has not been committed to him.

8. *There are special promises given to these officers.* They are given promises of present help and of future eternal rewards (Mt. 28:19-20; 1 Pet. 5:4). Those who take on this office without a divine call should not expect any special assistance for their work or any reward for their labours.

9. *The general rule of Scripture is that no one should take an office without a divine call* (see Heb. 5:4). Uzziah invaded the priesthood and was judged for it (2 Chr. 26:16-21). Jeremiah warned of taking a ministerial office without a call (Jer. 27: 9-15).

We can see, therefore, that whoever takes upon himself the office of pastor without a proper outward call, takes power and authority without divine warrant. This is the foundation of all disorder and confusion. Such a person seeks to destroy order in the church and threatens the church itself. However, three qualifications should be noted:

1. Some things that a pastor does in his office with special authority might also be done by those who are not pastors, if they are done in love. This includes moral duties like exhorting, admonishing, comforting, instructing, and praying with and for one another.

2. One who is not a pastor may exercise his gifts to edify others in an orderly way as he has opportunity. We do not approve, however, of a man regularly exercising the gift of preaching who has refused to undertake the minister's office and who has no intention of seeking it.

3. These rules concern ordinary circumstances. Extraordinary circumstances have their own rules.

Calling a pastor

The call to the pastoral office is an act and duty of the whole church. It is not an act of the state or the pope or of any individual person. The Lord Christ has committed the keys of the kingdom of heaven to the whole church. When a person is called to the pastoral office there needs to be an evaluation of his fitness, an election by the church and an ordination, when he is set apart for the work.

Evaluating fitness

It is never the church's duty to call unfit, unqualified, or unprepared people to this office. Doing so in the past has debased the ministry and nearly ruined the church. There are two ways to evaluate a person's fitness for this office:

1. By examining the qualifications already mentioned. The church is not to call or choose anyone for this office who is not known to them. They must have some experience of his general outlook and behaviour. He must not be a new believer or someone new to their church. He must be one who has a good reputation, even with outsiders. He must have given evidence of his faith, love, and obedience to Jesus Christ in the church. This is the chief trust Christ has given to his churches. To appoint an unfit officer dishonours Christ. Notice how in this matter churches are made the overseers of their own purity and edification. The church should not be denied the opportunity to make a proper judgment. Where personal knowledge is lacking, testimonies from trusted authorities must be given.

2. By a trial of his gifts for edification. These are the spiritual gifts that the Lord Jesus Christ grants and the Holy Spirit works in the minds of men to profit the church (1 Cor. 12:7-11). Every true church should be able to evaluate what gifts or men are suited to their own edification. Another resource is the advice of other elders and churches with which they share fellowship.

Election to office

Once a person's gifts have been tried and he is judged to be fit for the office, how is he to be elected? This is an act of the whole church, including the existing elders, if there are any. Where a pastor is being chosen for a church that already has other teachers, elders and officers, those already serving must give their approval. If there are no previous officers, as in the early church, then the election simply belongs to the brotherhood of believers.

Ordination

A person does not take office merely by the election of the church. He should also be set apart for the office with fasting and prayer. Prayer has not usually been neglected, but there has been less regard for fasting. However, both are necessary according to the example of the apostles (Acts 14:23). The practice of the laying on of hands should also be considered, although it is perhaps more difficult to prove its continuation after the extraordinary gifts ceased. However, it does seem appropriate for setting apart ordinary church officers although nobody should think that this alone conveys authority.

The task of ordination belonged to the extraordinary officers in the early church but today should be conducted by the elders or officers of the church where a person is to be ordained. If there are no officers in the church, they can seek the help of pastors and elders from other churches.

Some say that all authority of office is given by the laying on of hands through apostolic succession. This neglects the consent and call of the churches and neglects the rules, laws and order of Scripture. It is contrary to the whole nature of the evangelical church.

Is this process biblical?

Is it the mind and will of Christ to call persons to the office of pastor (or to any other office) by the election and choice of the church? What does the Bible teach?

In the Old Testament men were called to offices in the church in three ways. First, some were called extraordinarily and immediately by God himself. So Aaron was called to the priesthood and others, like Samuel, were called to be prophets. Second, some were called by physical inheritance. Thus the descendants of Aaron entered the priesthood without any other call. Third, some were called by the choice of the people. This was the call of all the ordinary elders and rulers of the church (cf. Deut. 1:13). The people were required first to examine the qualifications of those they might call. They were to look out for men known to be wise, understanding, righteous and God-fearing. They then presented them to Moses to be separated to the office. This is election to office. Yes, Exodus 18:25 does say that Moses chose the elders, but in the Bible it is common when something is done by many to say that it was done by them all or by their chief leader. For example, Numbers 21:21 says, 'Israel sent messengers', but in Deuteronomy 2:26 Moses says, 'I sent messengers'. We can conclude, then, that the people chose the elders under the guidance of Moses. This helps us decide how rightly to interpret passages like Acts 14:23.

In the New Testament, we see the first way of choosing officers repeated in the foundation of the evangelical church. Christ, by the Father, through the Spirit, called the apostles and evangelists. Those offices have now ceased. The second way (by natural inheritance) was utterly abolished. Only the third way remained for the ordinary continuation of the church:

1. The first example of choosing church officers is that of Matthias (Acts 1). It is a mix of the first and third ways. As a church officer he was chosen by the church. As an apostle, however, he was chosen directly by God. If the call to the office of apostle also involved the brotherhood of believers, how much more should any call to the ordinary offices! Notice the order of the proceedings:

    (1) the number of the church (the men) was about one hundred and twenty (Acts 1:15);

    (2) they were assembled in one place when Peter stood in their midst (v. 15);

    (3) Peter, in the name of the other apostles, announced the need to choose someone in Judas' place (vv. 16-22);

    (4) he limited the choice to those who were witnesses of the resurrection and who were present at Jesus' public ministry from the baptism of John;

    (5) of these, they had liberty to nominate any two for lots to be cast;

    (6) the whole multitude made their choice of two;

    (7) after prayer, the lots were cast and

(8) Matthias, by the common suffrage of the whole church, was added to the apostles. This was not done by the disciples apart from Peter and the apostles. It was done with them. Peter did nothing without the disciples. They did nothing without him.

2. The second example is the election of deacons in Acts 6. This was the first appointment of ordinary officers in the Christian church. At this time elders were not yet appointed, because the apostles were present. They did not exert their authority without consulting the church (v. 2). The entire church was assembled in one place (v. 3). The apostles would do nothing without their consent. After judging the matter they sought the church's approval before acting (v. 5). The apostles declared the qualifications for the office (v. 3). They committed the evaluation of fitness and choice, however, to the brethren. Once chosen, the officers were presented to the apostles to be set apart by prayer and the laying on of hands (v. 6).

3. The third example is the election of elders in Acts 14:23. The whole order of separating qualified people to the office of ministry (as bishops, elders, or pastors) is clearly presented: First, they were chosen by the people. The apostles, Paul and Barnabas, were present. They were presiding over and directing the action. They were also giving their approval. Second, a time of prayer and fasting was appointed for the church. Third, when they were so chosen, the apostles who were present solemnly prayed

for them. This completed their ordination. Fourth, this was done in each church. This means all the particular congregations gathered in those parts. The forming of a church always goes before the election and ordination of officers (see Tit. 1:5). Although a superficial reading might suggest that the appointment was simply an act of Paul and Barnabas, the Greek verb (*cheirotoneo*) used literally means 'to lift up' or 'stretch forth the hand'. In ancient Greek it was used when choosing, for example, a magistrate by common consent. In Acts 14:23, it might therefore truly be rendered, 'they appointed elders by the vote of the people'.

Why should the whole church be involved in the process?

1. Christ gives dignity and authority to the whole church. The church is the wife, the spouse, the bride, the queen. Jesus Christ is the husband and king of the church (see Ps. 45:9; Jn. 3:29; Rev. 21:9; 22:17; Mt. 25:1- 6). The officers and rulers of the church belong to her (1 Cor. 3:21-22). They act as stewards in the house (1 Cor. 4:1) and are servants of the church for Jesus' sake (2 Cor. 4:5). Notice also that the power of the keys is given to the whole church for binding and loosing (Mt. 18:17-18). The apostle Paul also makes this clear (1 Cor. 5:4-5; 2 Cor. 2:6). This right is seen in the commands that the apostles gave to the church regarding teachers and rulers of all sorts. In

many places they are told to discern and examine false prophets and to flee from them. They are told to test spirits and to examine closely those who pretend to have spiritual gifts or offices. They are told to reject preachers of false doctrine. They are told to provide testimony for those who desire to be officers (see Mt. 7:15-20; 1 Thes. 5:21; 1 Jn. 4:1; 2 Jn. 10-11).

2. The church is a voluntary society. By their own wills and free choice, people agree to join a church (2 Cor. 8:5). No church has more power or authority than another. They are all equal. A church is gathered by the authority of Christ alone. It has no right, power, privilege, rules, or duties except those given by Christ. It remains a church only while its members are subject to the commands of Christ. It is not like the dictatorships of the world where those who are born into them must live there and comply with their rules. A person only belongs to the church by free choice and consent. After the early years when there were extraordinary officers directly appointed by God, he gave the church authority, along with guiding rules and laws, to appoint their own officers.

3. This practice is scriptural and was observed in the ancient church. Its neglect in many periods of history has only caused damage to the church.

4. Objection to the people choosing their pastors and rulers has three weaknesses. First, it dishonours the wisdom of Christ. It says that Christ asks the people to do something they are not capable of doing. Second, it

supposes that the members of the church are in such a degenerate state that they are unfit for the task. If this is so, it is sad, and the church should be reformed. Third, it supposes that the church has no help in this duty. This should not be the case. The church has its own elders to help it. If these are lacking, it has help from the elders of other churches with which it shares fellowship.

Chapter 5
The office of pastor

We have discussed the way pastors are given to and installed in the church. We shall now discuss the work and duty of pastors.

The duty of preaching

The first duty of a pastor is to feed the flock by the diligent preaching of the Word. God promised to give the church pastors according to his own heart to 'feed [them] with knowledge and understanding' (Jer. 3:15). They do this by teaching or preaching the Word, and by no other way. Feeding is the essence of a pastor's work. He who does not, cannot, or will not feed the flock is no pastor. This is how Peter's responsibility to preach the gospel was explained to him (Jn. 21:15-17). According to the example of the apostles, pastors are to free themselves from all burdens, so that they may give themselves wholly to the Word and prayer (Acts 6:1-4). Their work is to labour in the Word and doctrine (1 Tim. 5:17). In so doing, they feed the flock over which the Holy Spirit has made them overseers (Acts 20:28).

This work and duty is essential to the office of pastor. He is not just required to preach every now and then when he finds the time. He must lay aside all other employments, even if they are lawful. This includes other duties in the church that might divert him from his work. He must give himself to the work and labour to the best of his ability. Without this, no pastor will be able to give an account of himself at the last day.

God requires no more of a man than he gives him ability to do. Weakness, sickness, or physical disability might hinder a pastor from doing his duty. Some might be hindered by age or by other serious troubles. In such cases it is their duty to give up the work. Men who only pretend to be pastors, who are unable to do the work and simply neglect it, are living in open defiance of the commands of Christ.

Sadly, there are some who despise preaching. Some have gone so far as to say that the work of preaching is unnecessary in the church. They reduce all religion to reading and ceremony. I suppose they might next attempt even to remove Christ from their religion! They make a good start in that direction by denying the need for the preaching of the gospel.

Here are a few things required in pastoral preaching:

1. *It requires spiritual wisdom and understanding of the mysteries of the gospel.* This is needed to declare to the church 'all the counsel of God' and 'the unsearchable riches of Christ' (see Acts 20:27; 1 Cor. 2:4-7; Eph. 3:8-11). The apostle Paul prays that all believers might have spiritual insight (Eph. 1:15-19). If the instructors do not have it, they cannot be useful in leading others on to

perfection. Failure here has made the ministry of many fruitless and useless.

2. *It requires that they have experienced in their own soul the power of the truth which they preach to others.* Without this, they will be lifeless and heartless in their work. Their labour, for the most part, will not profit others. A man only preaches a sermon well to others who has first preached it to his own soul. A man that refuses to eat the food he has prepared for others will scarcely make it appear appetizing to them. How does he know that it is not poison, if he has not tasted it? If the word does not dwell with power *in* us, it will not pass with power *from* us. No man lives in a more woeful condition than he who tries to get others to believe something that he does not truly believe himself. The lack of the power of the gospel truth in the souls of preachers has resulted in many lifeless sermons. Such sermons may use fine words, but they are dead and powerless. This is not the preaching of the gospel in the demonstration of the Holy Spirit. Some men show they are not called to preach as much by their preaching as by their failure to preach!

3. *It requires skill rightly to divide the Word* (2 Tim. 2:15). The preacher needs practical wisdom in his study of the Word so that he can find the appropriate food for the souls of his hearers. In this way each person in the church will receive exactly what they need.

4. *It requires a prudent and diligent consideration of the flock over which any man is set.* He must know their

51

strengths and weaknesses. He must know the areas where they have grown and where they still need to grow. He must know whether they need milk or strong meat. He must know where they are tempted and where they are doing their duty. He must know where there is spiritual decay and where there is spiritual thriving. He needs to know this not only about the church in general but also about the individual members. Neglect this, and he is just preaching at random. He is beating the air. He is preaching sermons that are not designed to bless the hearers. He is preaching general doctrines without specific application. He is telling men what they might believe instead of what they ought to believe. This makes the hearers weary of preaching.

5. *It requires zeal for the glory of God and compassion for the souls of men.* Where this is absent in the preaching of the Word, the life and soul of preaching is lost.

These things might seem obvious, but the lack of them has often ruined the ministry. The very naming of them challenges all pastors of churches to give themselves to the Word and prayer. They must stir up their graces and gifts for the discharge of their duty. Indeed, 'who is sufficient for these things?' Considering these things should stir up all ministers to pray fervently for God's help in their work. They can do nothing in their own strength. It should also warn them against any distraction from their work.

The duty of prayer

The second duty of a pastor to his flock is continual fervent prayer for them (Jas. 5:16; Jn. 17:20; Ex. 32:11; Deut. 9:18; 1 Sam. 12:23; 2 Cor. 13:7; Eph. 1:15-19; 3:14; Phil. 1:4; Col. 1:3; 2 Thes. 1:11). 'We will give ourselves continually to prayer' (Acts 6:4). Without this no man can preach as he ought or do any other duties of his pastoral office. From this a man may make the best assessment of his ministry to the flock. He who constantly, diligently and fervently prays for them will have a testimony of his sincerity in all other pastoral duties. Those who neglect this duty show a lack of sincerity. Whatever is done without this constant prayer has no value in the sight of Jesus Christ.

Here are some special areas for prayer:

1. Prayer should be offered for the success and blessing of the Word. To preach the Word and not to follow it with constant and fervent prayer for its success is an expression of disbelief in it. It neglects the goal. It is broadcasting the seed of the gospel at random.

2. Prayer should be offered regarding the particular temptations to which the church is being exposed. The temptations during a time of peace and tranquillity are different to those during times of trouble, persecution, distress and poverty. Pastors ought carefully to consider these things, knowing that many churches have been ruined and many souls have been lost for ever.

3. Prayer should be offered for the particular state and condition of all the members. Some may be spiritually

sick and diseased. Others may be tempted, afflicted, confused, and wandering out of the way. They may have fallen into sin or be troubled in spirit. Pastors ought to remember them. They should continually lift them up in their daily pastoral prayers.

4. Prayer should be offered for the presence of Christ by his Spirit in the meetings of the church. This alone gives life and power to our gatherings. Without this all the outward order and forms of worship are like a dead carcass. His presence is known by the blessing it gives to the heart and mind of the congregation. Pastors of churches are continually to pray for this. They will do so when they understand that all the success of their labours depends on it.

5. Prayer should be offered for preservation in faith, love and fruitfulness.

It is very important that those who take up the pastoral office understand how great and necessary is the work of constant and fervent prayer for their flocks. As they pray, they will find that their hearts and minds are filled with love. In consequence, they will be more diligent to do their other duties and to exercise all grace toward the church on all occasions.

The duty of administering ordinances

In addition to the authoritative teaching of the Word, pastors have been given the task of administering the seals of the covenant as stewards of the house of Christ. These ordinances are applications of the Word preached.

This includes three things in particular:

1. They are to decide the times and seasons to administer the ordinances for the church's edification. This is especially true of the frequency of the Lord's Supper, which should be often. It is the duty of the pastors to consider the circumstances of administration, including the time, place, frequency, order and decency.

2. They are to make sure that the administration closely conforms to the command of Christ. The gradual introduction of unbiblical rites and ceremonies changed the ordinance of the Lord's Supper into the idolatry of the mass! The glory and beauty of the ordinances lies in their compliance with the commands of Christ. The apostle Paul wrote, 'I have received of the Lord that which I also delivered unto you' (1 Cor. 11:23).

3. They are to take care that only those who are fit and worthy partake of holy things, according to the rule of the gospel. Those who want pastors to administer the ordinances to all without discretion deprive them of half their office and duty!

Observance of the Lord's Supper is an act of the local church and should therefore be administered only by its officers. Only Christ's stewards have authority in his house (1 Cor. 4:1; 1 Tim. 3:15; Mt. 24:45). Only those in office have the authority to represent Christ to the whole church and, thus, to feed the whole flock (Acts 20:28; 1 Pet. 5:2). We find no trace of any other practice in orderly churches in the Scriptures or the early church.

The duty of defending truth

Pastors must defend and preserve the truths of the gospel against all opposition. This is a principal goal of the ministry. It is a principal means of preserving the faith once delivered to the saints. We see this special duty for the pastors of churches in Paul's repeated and emphatic charges to Timothy (1 Tim. 1:3-4; 4:6-7,16; 6:20; 2 Tim. 1:14; 2:25; 3:14-17). He gave the same charge to the elders of the church of Ephesus (Acts 20:28-31). He says of himself that the 'glorious gospel of the blessed God' was committed to his trust (1 Tim. 1:11). This is true of all pastors of churches. They should all aim to give the same account that Paul gives of his ministry: 'I have fought a good fight, I have finished my course, I have kept the faith' (2 Tim. 4:7). The church is 'the pillar and ground of the truth'. Its ministry should be the same. The sinful neglect of this duty has led to heresies and errors infesting and ruining the church. Many of those who should have preserved the doctrine of the gospel have instead 'spoken perverse things, to draw away disciples after them'. Bishops, elders and public teachers have been ringleaders in heresies. This duty is especially needed at this time when all the fundamental truths of the gospel are under attack.

Here are the things required to defend the truth:

1. It requires a clear, sound, comprehensive knowledge of the entire doctrine of the gospel. All means should be used to gain this. It comes with diligent study of the Scripture. It comes with fervent prayer for illumination and understanding. Men cannot preserve for others what they are ignorant of themselves. Truth may be lost by weakness as well as by wickedness.

2. It requires love of the truth. We must look on truth as a pearl. Its value is beyond measure. It cannot be bought with any price. It is better than the entire world. Some part with the truth far too easily. They grow indifferent. There are many examples of evangelical truth that our fathers in the faith contended for and were ready to seal with their blood that today are disregarded or even opposed. If we do so, how can we pretend to be their successors? If ministers do not have the power of the truth in their own souls and a taste of its goodness we cannot expect them to do their duty.

3. It requires a fear of encouraging novel opinions. Vain curiosity has caused all sorts of trouble and damage to the church.

4. It requires learning and ability of mind to defend the truth against its adversaries. Pastors need this both to silence and to convince sceptics.

5. It requires solid establishment of the most important truths of the gospel. Pastors must be clear and thorough in their teaching and ministry. Men may betray the truth by the weakness of their pleas for it.

6. It requires pastors to keep a diligent watch over their own flocks. This is needed to protect the church both from false teachers outside and from the bitter root of error inside.

7. It requires the assistance of the elders and of the messengers of other like-minded churches. All the elders of all the churches must declare the faith which they all profess.

It is clear that learning, labour, study and abilities are required to discharge these duties. If a man is useful to the church in other things but weak in this he should walk and act carefully and humbly. He should also frequently seek the advice of those whom God has entrusted with more talents and greater abilities in this area.

The duty of evangelism

It is the duty of pastors to labour for the conversion of souls. Evangelism is a major responsibility of the church. When there are no more souls to be converted, the church on earth will be no more. God has designed his churches in the world to enlarge the kingdom of Christ and to spread the light of the gospel. They are to call the elect and to gather the sheep of Christ into his fold. The main way they do this is by preaching the Word, and this task is committed to the pastors of the churches. It is true that people may be, and often are, converted by means of those who are not church officers, because the gospel itself is the 'power of God unto salvation' whoever presents it (1 Cor.

14:24-25; Phil. 1:14-15, 18; 1 Pet. 4:10-11). Nonetheless, it is clear that the preaching of the glorious gospel is committed in the first place to the pastors of the churches.

The apostles and evangelists of the early church had the tasks of preaching the gospel, teaching those who were converted and gathering the disciples into churches. These churches had their own ordinary officers (pastors and teachers) who had the same work as the apostles and evangelists, but in their own particular flocks.

Here are some cases when pastors are to preach the Word for the conversion of souls:

1. They preach evangelistically when the unconverted come into their meetings. There are often converted church members and unconverted hearers in the same congregation. The pastor does not preach two sermons, one to the converted church members as their minister and another to the unconverted. Christ committed the preaching of the gospel to pastors, and he can use the same preaching simultaneously to meet the needs of both kinds of hearer.

2. They may occasionally preach in other places. The chief end of the gospel is the conversion of souls. Even the needs and edification of particular churches ought to give way to this. So, when there are great opportunities for evangelistic preaching, the pastors should pursue them. If the harvest is great and labourers few, it is lawful for a man to leave his regular pastoral duties in his church for a time, in order to do public evangelistic preaching.

Any particular church will understand that its edification must give place to the glory of Christ as a whole. The good shepherd will leave ninety-nine sheep to seek one that wanders. We may certainly leave a few for a little while to seek after a great multitude of wanderers. I heartily wish that we might have such opportunities!

The duty of counselling and care

It is the duty of pastors to be ready, willing and able to comfort, relieve and refresh the tempted, troubled and weary in their times of trial and desertion. Pastors must have 'the tongue of the learned that [they] should know how to speak a word in season to him that is weary' (cf. Is. 50:4). The Lord Jesus Christ in his priestly office in heaven is touched with our weaknesses. He was tempted during his life on earth and so knows how to help those who are tempted. His whole flock in this world is a company of tempted ones. Those with charge over this flock also should be aware of these weaknesses. They should try to help the tempted. There are always some people cast into darkness. Some at their conversion have a deep terror of the Lord. Some come under deep conviction. Some relapse into sin or fail in their duties. Some have great, painful and lasting afflictions. Some have to survive difficult circumstances. Some feel God has left them. Some are buffeted by Satan who places blasphemous thoughts in their minds. Men suffer various troubles that can perplex their souls almost to despair and death.

Here are some of the duties of pastors in counselling:

1. Pastors must be able rightly to understand the various cases they will encounter. This will not be done merely by collecting descriptions of various cases. In fact, rarely do we meet two cases that are the same. It requires skill, understanding and experience. It requires knowledge of the work of the Spirit of God on the souls of men. There is conflict between the flesh and the Spirit. It requires knowledge of the methods and wiles of Satan and his evil spirits. The pastor must understand these things. He must know how to give appropriate remedies for the various sicknesses. Although books on this topic may help, pastors and teachers are primarily equipped to counsel by diligent study of the Scriptures. They meditate on the Word. They pray fervently. They have their own spiritual experiences. Their souls face temptation. They observe God's dealings with others. They know the opposition to the work of grace. Without these things the pastor cannot fulfil his duties in counselling. This is why many have neglected it.

2. Pastors must pay attention to those who seek them out. They must give such people counsel and direction. They must not see this work as a distraction. It is a principal part of their office and duty. To discourage those who seek help is like hindering a lame man. It is a failure to express the care of Christ toward his flock (Is. 40:11).

3. Pastors must bear patiently and tenderly with the weaknesses of those who are troubled. Those who seek pastoral counsel may be ignorant, dull and slow to believe. This might be their natural state. It might also be exaggerated by their troubles. Their minds might be disordered and disquiet, filled with perplexing thoughts. If pastors are not patient, meek, and lowly toward them, such people might be turned away from Christ. There is no duty more important than this. There is no duty which more concerns Christ. Thus, pastors must exercise humility, patience, self-denial and spiritual wisdom.

4. Pastors must show compassion and be ready to share with all the members of the church in their trials and afflictions. Nothing renders pastors more like Jesus Christ. To represent him to the church is their principal duty and will encourage the church in all its troubles. Thus the apostle Paul said of himself, 'Who is weak, and I am not weak?' (2 Cor. 11:29). Unless men have this kind of compassion they cannot be called evangelical shepherds. They cannot call the sheep their own. Some want to be pastors to make a good living, disregarding the sufferings and temptations of the flock. Some want to be in such large churches that it is impossible to know the spiritual state of the majority of the flock. This is not the plan of Christ.

5. Pastors must care for the poor and visit the sick. This part of a pastor's duty is often neglected.

The duty of rule and fellowship among churches

The pastors have a leading role in the rule of the church. It is also the pastor's duty to lead the church in fellowship with other churches. Churches that share the same faith and profession should have fellowship, and the pastors should be concerned for the edification of all the churches. They might share letters offering mutual advice. They might offer congratulation or consolation to each other. They might help each other in calling officers. They might meet together to consult about joint concerns. It is the pastors' duty to take care of such matters.

The duty of a holy life

Without this last duty, nothing will be acceptable to the great Shepherd, Christ Jesus. The pastor must have a humble, holy, exemplary walk in all godliness and honesty. Scripture, the example of Christ and his apostles, and the witness of the early church all prove that this is necessary in a gospel ministry. It would be easy to fill a book with many sad examples from church history showing the damage caused to churches when unsuitable men were allowed to become pastors. If pastors are not exemplary in obedience and holiness, true religion will not continue and grow among the people. A church will be spiritually impoverished if it is led by a man who is superficial and profane in his habits, who is corrupt and barren in his own spiritual life or who is covetous, oppressive and contentious. If he cannot care for his own life or that of his family, he will not be able to care properly for the church. It is even worse if he is openly immoral.

We need to study the apostle Paul's description of the qualifications for elders in 1 Timothy 3:2-7 and Titus 1:6-9. Here also are a few other things to have in mind:

1. Any consideration of this matter will make the wisest and best of men cry out, 'Who is sufficient for these things?' The pastor's call to the ministry will be the only thing that will justify him in pursuing the office of pastor. No sense of insufficiency will discourage him if the Lord Christ has truly called him. When Christ calls a man to fulfil a duty, he gives him the strength to do it. When the pastor says, 'Who is sufficient for these things?' Christ answers, 'My grace is sufficient.'

2. Although the qualifications for pastors are clear, they are often overlooked. The present ruin of religion in its power, beauty and glory comes from this neglect. Multitudes take this office who are not fit for it and do not perform the duties required in it. The saying will always be true, 'Like priest, like people'.

3. An account must be given to Christ at the last day, and he will evaluate ministers based on these scriptural grounds. Those who want to give an account of their ministry with joy and confidence, and not with grief and confusion, should keep in mind what Christ requires of pastors.

4. No man can be the pastor of more than one church, especially if the churches are far distant from each other. Sober minded men will agree, because they know the account that each pastor must give to Christ. Of course, it is as foolish to have ten churches and never do the duty of a true pastor to them as it is to have only one church and never do the duty of a true pastor to it!

5. All churches need to consider the weight and burden on their pastors and teachers as they discharge their office. This will make them pray fervently for their pastors. It will also make them want to provide for their needs, so they can be without trouble and care for the things of this life.

6. Although it may seem impossible for any one man to be gifted and qualified to fill this office, we need to remember that the goal of any pastor is the edification of the church. If this is accomplished, he has done his duty. This can happen even if some of his gifts are not the strongest. If a man proves to be particularly weak in any one area, the church might call someone to assist him who is stronger in that area. This can help to edify the church. This can also be done when a pastor cannot do some part of his duty due to age or illness. The edification of the church must be the first consideration.

7. Sometimes a church may have a pastor who is not qualified for office or who neglects his duties. He may not be able to preach the Word or he may not be willing to work hard at studying the Scriptures and prayer. His

life may be so defective that his sins are a stumbling block to others. No church has the power to call an unqualified man to the office of pastor and when such unfit men are admitted to the office of pastor, their work is meaningless. These men ought to be challenged and convicted by the rule and law of Christ. If people accept them, they become partakers of their sin and so bring themselves under judgment. If such pastors are not removed or reformed, then it is the duty of those who care about their own edification and salvation to leave the fellowship of that church. They should then join a church that better provides for their growth. It would be the highest folly to say that a disciple of Christ is obliged to stay in such churches.

Three more questions about pastors

Can a man be ordained as a pastor or minister without relation to any particular church?

It is sometimes answered that a man may be ordained as a pastor to the catholic (universal) church, although he is not related to any particular flock or congregation. It is argued that this might be done, for example, when a man is being sent out as a missionary. My answer is:

1. Certainly, a man with the spiritual gifts for the preaching of the gospel may be set apart by prayer and fasting for that work. This is done when he is called in an orderly

manner in the providence of God. Such a person has the gifts for edifying others (1 Pet. 4:10-11; 1 Cor. 14:12). He should be set apart by special prayer (Acts 13:1-3). There should also be a public testimony that the person is undertaking the work of preaching. This should be made first to the fellowship of churches, so they might receive him. In the early church they used letters of recommendation (1 Cor. 16:3; 2 Cor. 3:1; 3 Jn. 9). This is for the safety of those among whom he might preach. It guards against false teachers. The early church did not allow a person who lacked this testimony regularly to preach the gospel. It should not be allowed today in the fellowship of churches.

2. Such people may be used in the establishment of new churches and might then be installed as pastors in these churches.

3. However, no church has the power to ordain men as ministers for other people. A man can only be ordained as a pastor or elder for a particular church and by that church. To appoint men to an office without a call to a particular church would be contrary to the practice of the apostles. They only ordained ordinary officers to serve in particular churches. Over these churches such men took proper charge and care (Acts 14:23; Tit. 1:5). Nowhere in Scripture do we find ordinary officers who are not connected to particular churches (see Acts 20:28; Phil. 1:1; Rev. 2-3). This practice was unknown in the early church and the period immediately following. It would

neglect the essential role of the election of the people in ordination. The titles elder and pastor necessarily imply a relationship to a particular church, a people, a flock. To make a man a pastor who has no church is like making a man a father who has no child, or a husband who has no wife. Those called, set apart, and ordained must take up certain duties. None of these duties can be taken up except in particular churches. To do otherwise is irregular. The duty of ruling, in particular, is an essential part of the pastoral office. A man cannot rule who has no one to rule over.

May a pastor move from one congregation to another?

This question arose early in church history, as some bishops tried to move from smaller churches to larger and more prosperous ones. We cannot deny, however, that there may be good reasons for a pastor to move from one congregation to another. The purpose of all particular churches is to support the edification of the universal church. Proper consideration should be given to the particular people, places and times. If there is to be a transition, the churches concerned should give their free consent to the move, and they should consult other churches and elders with whom they are in fellowship.

May a pastor voluntarily resign and remain in the church as a private member?

Early in church history we find resignation discouraged, though not judged unlawful. No general rule can be established. Here, however, are a few guidelines:

1. It is not right for a man to resign merely on account of some weakness due to age, sickness, or physical problems. No man can do more than he is physically able to do. The church should be satisfied if a pastor is doing the best with the abilities he has. However, resignation would be appropriate if the man was not able to fulfil his duties, for example because of incurable mental decline.

2. It is not lawful for a man to resign merely because he is weary and despondent in the face of opposition. A pastor is called to endure this for the good and edification of the flock. He must not faint in the warfare to which he is called.

3. It is sometimes lawful to resign if there are incurable divisions in the church. Such conflict obstructs edification. Obstructions might not be removed while the man is in office, even if it is not his fault. This holds only if there is no other way to settle the conflict. Perhaps, instead, those causing the division can be cast out of the church. Or, the church might withdraw fellowship from them. If the division results in distinct parties due to settled principles, opinions and practices, they might separate into two fellowships. In such cases, a pastor

might not have to resign. All things are to be done for edification.

4. It might be lawful for a pastor to resign if the church is wholly negligent in its duty in providing, according to their abilities, for the outward needs of the pastor and his family. This cannot be determined without knowing the specific circumstances.

5. Finally, a man may resign if he cannot cheerfully and comfortably discharge his office. This is especially true if the issue is a point of conscience. The church may be unwilling to obey a duty which Christ has commanded. The Lord Christ lays no yoke on the neck of his servants to remain as pastors in such churches. Such a person may peaceably lay down his office. He might remain in the church as a private member or he might take the care of another church where he may serve as pastor for their edification with a clear conscience.

Chapter 6
The office of teacher

The Lord Christ has given to his church 'pastors and teachers' (Eph. 4:11). He has, 'set in the church first apostles, secondarily prophets, thirdly teachers' (1 Cor. 12:28). There were 'prophets and teachers' at the church in Antioch (Acts 13:1).

The 'teacher' cannot be only a general name for one who taught others whether regularly or only occasionally. It is true that in the early church all who had spiritual light and the gifts of knowledge and utterance taught and instructed others (1 Pet. 4:8-11). The pagan philosopher Celsus even criticised the early Christians, because common people, like weavers and shoemakers, taught among them. Nevertheless, the verses above show that there was a distinct office of teacher and that such people were set apart for that duty and joined in the public ministry of the church. It is also the case that the Greek *didaskalos* ('teacher') is not used in the New Testament except for a teacher with authority.

There are various views on what the Bible says about the office of teacher.

View 1: the teacher is the same office as pastor

Some suggest that the same people are both pastors and teachers. Men tend to go to extremes. The Roman church went to the extreme of adding unbiblical offices. In reaction to this, some have gone to the opposite extreme. They deny and reject some offices that do have biblical warrant and which have been given by God to edify the church. With regard to the distinct office of teacher, consider the following:

1. *There were catechism teachers in the early church.* In the second century at Alexandria there were teachers who were not pastors. They did not administer the ordinances. Their public work was to teach all who came to them, both believers and unbelievers. They explained and taught the Christian religion. They defended it against pagan opponents, atheists and philosophers. This would not have been practised in the church at this time unless it was by divine institution. This is the same as the catechism teacher (literally) that Paul refers to in Galatians 6:6. He is one who labours constantly in the work of catechising, teaching and preaching. He has people who are being taught and catechised by him. This is how he makes his living. This is not a reference to the pastor of the church.

2. *There is a distinction made between the offices of a pastor and a teacher* (Eph. 4:11: 'Some pastors and teachers'). The apostle does not say 'pastors *or* teachers', which is what he should have done if he meant that these were

the same person or the same office. He makes a point of naming teachers, a better known term, after pastors rather than before. Where church officers are listed in the New Testament, they are never given more than one name. Although pastors, bishops and presbyters are the same office, the Bible does not say that there were in the church bishops *and* presbyters; if it did, we would have to acknowledge that these were two distinct offices, just like bishops and deacons in Philippians 1:1. Finally, the words pastor and teacher are not synonymous. All pastors are teachers, but not all teachers are pastors. We cannot exchange one term for the other.

3. *Teachers have distinct duties assigned to them.* The gifts of teaching and exhorting are distinguished in Romans 12:7-8. If they have special work by virtue of their office, then their office is distinct also.

4. *Scripture makes a distinction between teachers and prophets* (1 Cor.12:28). They are also mentioned separately in the church at Antioch (Acts 13:1). Pastors have now taken the place of prophets.

From all these considerations, it appears that teachers in the Scripture were church officers, distinct from pastors. They are distinguished from them by their name and by their particular work carried out in the church.

View 2: the teacher is a distinct office without other duties

Some suggest that teachers are a distinct office, but that the office is confined to teaching only. Therefore teachers have no role in rule or in the administration of the sacraments. This appears to have been the practice of the churches after the apostles. They ordinarily had catechism teachers and teachers in assemblies like schools. These, however, were not called to the whole work of pastoral ministry. It seems therefore, that it is lawful for a church to choose, call, and set apart people to the office of teacher, without giving them duties in rule of the church or the administration of the ordinances of worship. This is already the practice of many, though they do not do it in an orderly way. If they did, we might recover the original design of this office. In this view, a teacher has no more right to rule or administer the ordinances than a Jewish rabbi had to offer sacrifices in the temple. Nevertheless, one who is called to be a teacher might, at the same time, also be called to be an elder. And a teaching elder has the power to do all the duties committed to him. Now the person who is called to be a teacher and who also serves as an elder must still give special attention to the work of teaching.

View 3: the teacher is a distinct office of the same kind as pastor

The view that I tend to prefer supposes that a teacher is a distinct office in the church, but it is of the same kind as that of a pastor. The distinction between the two is one of degrees.

Teachers are joined with pastors in the same order, as if they were associates in office (Eph. 4:11). Teachers are also associated with prophets (1 Cor. 12:28; Acts 13:1). They have a specific work that is of the same general nature as that of pastors (Rom. 12:7). The teaching and preaching they do is essentially the same as that of pastors. They are said 'to minister [Greek: *leitourgesai*] to the Lord' in the church (Acts 13:1-2), which would include administration of all the ordinances.

Three observations

1. There may be teachers in the church who are called only to the work of teaching, without any interest in rule or the administration of the sacraments. These would seem to be like the ones mentioned in Galatians 6:6. They are called 'catechists'. In 1 Corinthians 4:15 there is also a reference to instructors (literally, of those that are young; *paidagogoi*). So, we know that these kinds of teachers existed in the early church. This was much needed in the days when the churches were great and numerous. If the whole rule of the church is given to the pastor, and the church grows very large, how could he handle all his duties? This would be impossible for any one man. This is why it pleased the Lord to appoint a distinct office, associated with pastors, to help in the discharge of the various parts of their duty. The same is true with deacons. They were appointed to take care of the poor and the outward needs of the church, without

any interest in rule or teaching. So also with elders, as we shall see. They were ordained to help and assist in rule, without any call to preach or administer the sacraments. And so it is with teachers. They were appointed to teach and instruct but not to rule or administer the other ordinances. Pastors have the whole duty of making sure that the church is edified, but they are supplied with assistants in every part of their work. This way they can comfortably get their job done. If this design were observed in churches, they would avoid many problems. The order and edification of the church would greatly increase.

2. The person who is particularly called to be a teacher (distinct from a pastor) may also, at the same time, be called to be an elder. He would then be a teaching elder. Where an officer has both the right to rule as an elder and the power to teach or preach the gospel, he is essentially a pastor.

3. Even so, there yet remains a distinction between pastors and teachers. The distinction consists in the different gifts that each has received. The church needs to consider this as it calls them. It also relates to how they exercise their gifts in their office, as they do the special work assigned to them.

How many pastors and teachers should a church have?

Given this discussion, one might ask: How many pastors and teachers are needed to edify a church? Can there be many of each in a particular church? Here is my response:

1. If we are talking about teachers as discussed under the second view (teachers only), a church might and ought to have as many as it finds necessary for its edification. If we observed this, it would prevent the problem of men regularly preaching who hold no church office. Those ordained to the ministry have the right and the duty to be constant in preaching. I do not think it is justified for other men to give themselves up to the regular work of teaching, by preaching the gospel, who were never set apart for that task by the church.

2. Since there were many elders in each church (Acts 14:23; 20:17, 28; Phil. 1;1; Tit. 1:5), it follows that if all elders were of the same kind, there would be many pastors in the same church. However, the Scripture mentions various types of elder and these could include the pastor who especially feeds the flock, the teaching elder, and the ruling elder. This issue is explained in Chapter 7.

3. Very early it became the practice for there to be one pastor in each church. He was distinguished even when he had many elders assisting him in rule and teaching and many deacons ministering in the things of this life. By this, the order of the church was preserved and its

authority was represented. Still, I will not deny that it might be possible for there to be many pastors in the same church – all equal in power – if the edification of the church requires it.

4. This simple biblical order was soon compromised. After the time of the early church, a new form of church government arose that was never appointed by Christ. This happened as many churches came together under one leader. It led to the episcopal system which degenerated and resulted in confusion in the name of order.

5. We need to return to the original congregational form of church order. This also means returning to the original order for church officers. There should be one pastor or bishop in one church who is assisted in his duties by many elders, including both teaching and ruling elders.

6. If there are many teaching elders in any church, an equality in office and power is to be preserved. This does not deny the special role for the pastor. It also does not deny the need for someone to preside in church meetings to observe proper order. It also does not deny particular roles for individuals that might come with gifts, age, abilities, prudence and experience.

Chapter 7
The office of ruling elder

The rule and government of the church is in the hands of the elders. They execute the authority of Christ in the church and all that belongs to the care, inspection, oversight, rule and instruction of the church belongs to them. All elders have rule, and none has rule in the church except elders.

'Elders' is a name derived from the Jews. In all languages 'elders' generally refers to older men. Respect and reverence is due to them by the law of nature and the command of Scripture, unless they forfeit this privilege by levity or wickedness. Ancient people judged that such older men were the best fitted for rule. In this way, the name of 'elders' came to be given to those who ruled or presided over others in any way but in the Scripture secular rulers are never called 'elders'. The highest officers of the Christian church are called elders, and this also includes the apostles (1 Pet. 5:1; 2 Jn. 1; 3 Jn. 1; see Acts 21:18; 1 Tim. 5:17). Some of them, on occasion, were called by titles like bishops, pastors, teachers, ministers, or guides. When it came to matters of rule, however, their authority came from the fact that they were elders (cf. Acts 20:17,28).

Church power is called 'the keys of the kingdom'. This term was used for power in the families of the kings (Is. 22:22). It was used by our Saviour to describe the giving of power to others, under the name 'the key of David' (Rev. 3:7; Mt. 16:19). These keys are of two sorts: (1) the key of order, meaning the spiritual authority given to elders or pastors to preach the word, to administer the sacraments, and to bind and loose the consciences of men doctrinally; and (2) the key of rule, which is the authority to govern and exercise the discipline of the church. These are two distinct powers (teaching and ruling) and there are correspondingly two sorts of elders. Some elders are called to both teaching and ruling, and others are called to ruling only. The roles of pastors and teaching elders have been described in Chapters 5 and 6. We now look at the Scripture evidence and duties of ruling elders.

The need for ruling elders

Here are some general considerations, which will be followed by examination of some key texts of Scripture:

1. The work of rule in the church is distinct from the pastoral role of preaching the Word and the administration of the sacraments. Spiritual rule is absolutely necessary and required by Scripture to promote peace, purity and order in the church (see Acts 20:28; Rom. 12:8; 1 Cor. 12:28; 1 Tim. 3:5; 5:17; Heb. 13:7,17; and Rev. 2-3). The work of rule is to watch over the conduct of the members of the church with authority. This includes exhorting,

comforting, admonishing, reproving, encouraging and directing them as the circumstances require. The gifts needed are diligence, wisdom, courage and seriousness. The pastoral work, by contrast, is principally to 'declare the whole counsel of God', to 'divide the word aright', or to 'labour in word and doctrine'. Pastors make general and particular applications of the Word, in all seasons and on all occasions. This requires spiritual wisdom, knowledge, sound judgment, experience and utterance. It is improved by continual study of the Word and prayer.

2. Different gifts are required for distinct duties. Gifts are given to correspond with all duties required (Eph. 4:7; 1 Cor. 12:4,7-10; Rom. 12:6-8; 1 Pet. 4:10). Differing gifts are the first foundation of differing offices and duties. In particular, different gifts are required for the work of pastoral teaching, on the one hand, and practical rule, on the other. This is a reasonable conclusion, given that the works are so different. We also find it is true in experience. Some men are gifted for teaching the Word and pastoral feeding who are not as gifted in rule. Likewise, some men are gifted for rule but not for preaching. Indeed, it is very seldom that both gifts are strong in the same person. Those who are ready to take all things on themselves are usually fit for nothing! Most of those who take on both duties end up neglecting one or the other. Too often, pastoral preaching is neglected in favour of rule. This neglect might be avoided if we

would realise that the rule of the church is given to some as a special duty.

3. Although some men are gifted for both duties, there is a basis for distinct offices when different works and duties are required. We see a parallel case in Acts 6:2-4. The apostles needed to concentrate on the Word and prayer for the spreading of the gospel and the edification of the church. In the wisdom of the Holy Spirit, others were given responsibility to ensure that the church fulfilled its biblical duty to care for the poor.

4. The work of the ministry of prayer and preaching of the Word, along with the administration of the sacraments, is more than enough to absorb the whole man who is called to the pastoral office. The excellence and greatness of the work is such that the apostle Paul exclaimed, 'Who is sufficient for these things?' (2 Cor. 2:16). The manner of its performance adds to its weight. The mind must be intense in the exercise of faith, love, zeal and compassion that is required. The pastor must diligently consider the flock to know how properly to feed them. He must give constant attention to the effect of the Word in the consciences and lives of men. This will, for the most part, take up their whole time and strength. Our rule is plain (see 1 Tim. 4:12-16).

5. If pastors and teachers, called to the ministry of the Word, are given help in government by ruling elders, this does not mean that they are relieved of the right to rule the church. The right and duty of rule is inseparable

from the office of elders but they should exercise it in a way consistent with their more excellent work. So it was in the founding of the first eldership of the church of Israel (Ex. 18:17-23). Before this, Moses had the sole rule and government of the people. In the creation of the eldership for his assistance, the right and exercise of his power was not diminished. Likewise, when the apostles established elders in every church, this did not diminish their authority. So also, when they appointed deacons to care for the poor, this did not remove their right to exercise this duty, as their other work permitted (see Gal. 2:9-10). The apostle Paul, in particular, manifested this concern in his collection for the poor in all the churches.

6. For any particular church to be complete there must be more than one elder in it. This is a foundational truth. It does not mean, however, that we can set a specific number of elders that every church should have. The number of elders must be proportional to the size and scope of the work. Elders should not be appointed only for show but to ensure that there are enough elders to do the work that is required.

The teaching of 1 Timothy 5:17

We need to establish some guidelines for interpreting this verse. First, we must interpret it in the context of what other Scriptures teach about offices and church government. Second, we must accept the plain meaning of this verse. It holds no spiritual mystery. The literal sense of the words should be reasonably understood. A reasonable reader, with no prejudices and who never heard of controversy over ruling elders, would come to a clear conclusion. There are two sorts of elders. There are some, the pastors and teachers, who labour in the Word and doctrine, and there are others, the ruling elders, who do not. Those who strain their wits to avoid this plain interpretation do so out of prejudice.

There are those who oppose our interpretation of 1 Timothy 5:17. They attempt to make exceptions to the obvious sense and interpretation of the words. They think they can avoid the force of these words by pretending they are capable of another sense. But every testimony of the Scripture has one determinate sense. If there is more than one interpretation suggested then we must examine the meaning and use of the words, consider the context, compare other Scripture passages, and apply the analogy of faith to reach a conclusion. Our adversaries fail to do this. They do not even agree among themselves in interpreting this verse. Scarcely any two of them share the same opinion.

Without attempting to contest various interpretations I will make one logical argument for interpreting this passage:

1. Preaching elders, though they rule well, are not worthy of double honour, unless they labour in Word and doctrine.

2. But there are elders who rule well that are worthy of double honour, though they do not labour in the Word and doctrine.

3. Therefore, there are elders who rule well who are not teaching and preaching elders. That is, they are ruling elders only.

Some suggest that the word 'especially' (*malista*) does not indicate a distinction but only a description and would render the verse 'The elders that rule well are worthy of double honour, *especially considering that* they labour in word and doctrine.' This interpretation is not supported by any of the old translations or the use of the word in the New Testament, where it is always used to distinguish one person or thing in comparison to others. For example, see Philippians 4:22: 'All the saints salute you, chiefly [*malista*] they that are of Caesar's household'; two sorts of saints are clearly expressed, the saints in general and those of Caesar's household. Other examples are Acts 20:38, Galatians 6:10, 1 Timothy 5:8, 2 Timothy 4:13, 2 Peter 2:9-10 and Acts 26:3. Other ancient authors use the word in the same way as it is used in the New Testament.

Others suggest that the word 'labour' (*kopiontes*) refers to a particular kind of especially strenuous work in the ministry, for example an evangelist who was not confined to one place but travelled throughout the world to preach the gospel. However, this is a general word that describes the duty of all pastors and teachers and indeed anyone in the service of God. It is applied to the prophets and teachers of the Old Testament (Jn. 4:38). It is applied to the labour of women and others in serving the church (Rom. 16:6,12). There is no evidence that it was used especially of evangelists who travelled throughout the world to preach the gospel, while it is certainly used of locally-based elders in 1 Thessalonians 5:12: 'We beseech you, brethren, to know them which labour among you.'

There are, therefore, two duties mentioned and commanded in 1 Timothy 5:17. They are ruling well and labouring in the Word and doctrine. Both these duties are committed to one sort of elder (pastors or teachers). Only one of these duties (ruling) is the responsibility of another sort of elder (ruling elders). The intention of the apostle is that when each does his duty both are worthy of double honour.

Some might also object that material support belongs to the term 'double honour'. Does this mean that the church should give material support to those elders whose work is rule only? I would answer, 'Yes', but under the following circumstances: (1) the church is able to provide for them; (2) their work takes up all the whole or greater part of their time; and (3) they stand in need of it.

The teaching of Romans 12:6-8

Amongst the different gifts given by God to the church, this passage includes ruling. The verb *proistemi* means 'to rule with authority by virtue of office'. In noun form, it means 'one who presides over others with authority'. There is a particular gift to discharge this duty which must be done with diligence (v. 8). This ruler is distinguished from those who exhort and teach and is therefore our ruling elder. Although the passage is primarily dealing with gifts rather than offices, gifts do nothing more than prepare men to exercise their calling. If a man has received a gift of teaching but is not called to the office of teacher then he is not required or encouraged to do public teaching. To rule requires a special relationship between the ruler and those ruled. This is the relationship of an office. It requires that the ruler be above those who are ruled. 'Obey them that are over you in the Lord.' In the church this can only be done because he has been appointed to that office.

Some may suggest that 'he that ruleth' simply refers to the pastor or teacher, the teaching elder. However, the duties of exhorting and ruling are clearly distinguished in this passage. Rule is not the principal work of the pastor. It does not require his constant attention. His focus should be given to labouring in the Word and doctrine.

The teaching of 1 Corinthians 12:28

This passage lists both ordinary and extraordinary offices and officers in the church (apostles, prophets, teachers). There is also mention of extraordinary gifts (miracles, healings and tongues). Finally mention is made of 'helps' and 'government'. Most agree that the term 'helps' refers to the deacons in the church. The term 'governments' refers to governors or rulers. Note that God has placed them in the church as distinct from 'teachers'. So it ought to be. Some object that these are gifts and not offices. If these are ordinary gifts meant to continue in the church, however, someone must exercise them, and this means that there is a distinct office of rule in the church.

Learning from the original order of the Jerusalem church

The original order of these things is plain in the Scriptures. At the start, the apostles had all church power and church office. When the Jerusalem church was small they acted in all things with consent of the whole multitude (see Acts 1:15-26). When the number of believers increased the apostles could not attend to all the duties. So, by the guidance of the Holy Spirit, they added the office of deacon to care for the poor of the church. It is also evident that, in a similar manner, when the apostles could no longer attend personally to the rule of the church without neglecting their labour in the Word and prayer, they appointed elders to help in this task.

These elders in the Jerusalem church are first mentioned in Acts 11:30. By this time, they were already well known and had been in the church for some time. They are mentioned along with the apostles and are distinct from the church itself (Acts 15:2,4,6,22; 16:4; 21:18). Now, the apostles were teaching elders, having both teaching and rule committed to them (1 Pet. 5:1; 2 Jn. 1). The elders they appointed were distinct from them and there is no mention of them teaching and preaching. The apostles reserved this to themselves (Acts 6:2-4). While the apostles were in Jerusalem, giving themselves wholly to the Word and prayer, it is improbable that they would have appointed teaching elders. Nevertheless, it is plain that there were many elders, and they are everywhere described as joining with the apostles in the rule of the church.

The nature of church authority

Church authority is often misunderstood, disputed, ignored or abused.

1. There is an authority given to some people in the church that is not given to the body as a whole. The church is democratic in the sense that the people have liberty and must offer consent in government. However, when the church takes a vote on a matter, it is not an independent executive decision but should only be to express consent and obedience to what the leadership has decided.

2. No one can dispute that Christ has instituted such authority and rule in his church. Christ has called some to rule and others, like sheep and lambs, to be ruled. They are commanded to obey them, to follow them and to submit to them in the Lord as those who are over them. These things are frequently repeated in the Scripture. When due respect is not given to those in authority, the result is only confusion and disorder. At times the people judge that the power of the keys is committed to them only. They believe that their elders can only lead as they approve or as seems reasonable to them. They do not acquiesce to the authority of their elders in anything. This is an evil apt to grow in churches. When this happens, it overthrows all that beautiful order which Jesus Christ has ordained.

3. This authority in the rulers of the church is not autocratic, despotic, or absolute, but is only a service to

Christ's church. When leaders take on autocratic power in the church it is destructive of the kingly office of Christ. It is contrary to the express commands of Scripture and is condemned by the apostles (see Is. 33:22; Jas. 4:12; Mt. 17:5; 23:8-11; Lk. 22:25-26; 2 Cor. 1:24; 1 Cor. 3:21-23; 2 Cor. 4:5; 1 Pet. 5:1-3).

4. Rule in the church is limited to spiritual matters concerning the authority of Christ, his law, and the liberty of the church. The apostle Paul expressly affirms this in 2 Corinthians 10:4-6. It concerns the souls and consciences of men and so is quite distinct from other authorities in human society. Its purpose is the glory of God. It seeks to guide and direct the minds and souls of men to live for God and come to enjoy him. It is to be exercised according to the word, command and direction of Christ himself alone. Its actions of binding and loosing, remitting and retaining sin and of opening and shutting the kingdom of heaven are exclusively spiritual and do not concern political matters.

5. This spiritual rule in church government was lost when unsuitable and worldly men became leaders of churches. They did not understand or recognise spiritual leadership and wanted instead the worldly advantages of profit, honour and praise. As a result, the biblical pattern of church government was replaced by a worldly organisation wielding political power. This is completely foreign to the purpose of Christ.

The manner of ruling

Church officers need spiritual wisdom and understanding to govern according to the law of Christ. It is only Christ's law that should govern the church, and it is therefore essential that they know how to apply that law in various circumstances for the edification of the church and all its members. Thus, they represent Christ's holiness, love, care, compassion and tenderness towards his church. We have already discussed how this wisdom is both given as a spiritual gift and also acquired by the duties of prayer, meditation and study of the Word. It is a very practical type of wisdom. It requires diligence, care, watchfulness and spiritual courage. Some people have to be admonished. Some have to be rebuked sharply. Some have to be excommunicated. This is another reason why there should be many elders in each church. Seldom is one man qualified for the whole work of rule. Some may have a good understanding of the law but a natural tenderness and modesty. They are hesitant to reprove and censure. Others may not have as strong an ability to understand the law, but they are ready and bold to apply it when required. Thus, all elders, with their various gifts, are to be helpful to each other in the common work to which they are called. Those who lack these gifts are not called to this work, or any part of it.

It is important to remember that it is Christ's authority that is committed to the elders (2 Cor. 10:8). This authority does not reside in the rulers of the church in the same way that the power of a king resides in his person. It is a power to serve as instruments. It is the authority of Christ himself that affects men's consciences. It is by him that men are bound or loosed in heaven and earth, have their sins remitted or retained. It is this alone that makes men respect the ministry of the church.

The rule of the church is specially designed to represent the holiness, love, compassion, care and authority of Christ towards his church. When the officers and rulers of the church do not attempt to display these virtues of Christ, they completely miss the purpose of church government. Sometimes men are domineering. They are visibly elated to be placed above others. They get angry and passionate. They introduce rules and procedures which they have created, without considering in the least what Christ requires. When this happens it reflects the highest dishonour imaginable upon Christ himself and spoils the reputation of the church. How often have Christians failed to show the holiness, wisdom, love and compassion of Christ in the administration of church rule and discipline! Paul describes the church's censure of a sinner as a matter of the deepest sorrow and concern (2 Cor. 12:21). With such sorrow and pity we demonstrate the compassion of the Lord Christ towards the souls of sinners.

The standard of ruling

The standard for rule by the elders in the church is the holy Scripture alone. The Lord Christ is the only lawgiver of the church. All his laws are recorded in the Scripture. No other standard can be used in church rule. If a church makes a thousand rules and laws of government, none of them has the least power to require men's obedience. They are only valuable to the degree that they contain the law of Christ and originate from it. Secular judges in the courts must make decisions based on the law of the land. If they fail to do so, their decision is invalid and ought to be reversed. If they were to introduce laws not approved by the nation this would be criminal, and they should be punished. So it is in the kingdom of Christ. The task for the elders of the church is to apply Christ's laws to particular cases and occasions. To make or bring in other laws is to usurp his kingly dominion.

The acts of ruling

There are three areas of responsibility:

1. *Admitting and excluding members.* These are both acts of church power and authority. They can only be exercised by the elders, given that the church is healthy and complete with its proper officers. A voluntary society has the right to accept members and to exclude members. This is true of the church, even before officers are installed in it. It may admit fit persons into membership and remove those who are not fit. When elders and rulers are installed, according to the mind of Christ, peculiar authority is given to them in the admission and exclusion of members. The key of rule is given to them, and it is applied with the consent of the whole church.

2. *Directing the church for the glory of God and for its own edification.* This includes ensuring that the members (1) have mutual, intense and special love to one another; (2)

live holy lives; (3) are helpful to other members of the church and to those outside as opportunity allows; and (4) fulfil their responsibilities as members of the church.

3. *Managing the meetings of the church.* This should be done according to the general rules of the Word and common sense so that 'all things may be done decently and in order'. This includes arranging the time and place for these meetings, regulating what is said and done in them, and planning for special occasions.

All elders are responsible for the rule and government of the church, whether they are teaching elders or ruling elders. All acts of rule are by common decision of the eldership. However, in the wisdom of God, ruling elders have a particular office and duty to attend to the matters described. This allows the teaching elders to concentrate on their especial responsibilities while ensuring that proper care is taken to see that the commands of Christ are observed by and among all the members of the church.

The duties of ruling elders

Here are some examples of the duties of ruling elders:

1. They are to watch diligently over the conduct and conversation of all the members of the church. They want to see the members blameless, without offence and exemplary. They want the members to be holy, living according to the command of Christ, to honour the gospel, and to present a consistent witness. They

are placed in the church to instruct, admonish, charge, exhort, encourage and comfort, as they see need. They are to do this with courage and diligence.

2. They are to watch for signs of differences and divisions. Such divisions are contrary to the love which Christ required to be present among his disciples. He called this his own 'new commandment'. The rule of the church principally consists in the observance of this law of love. We must consider the weakness, the passions and the temptations of men. Even among the best, men are apt to provoke and exasperate one another. Thus, this duty or part of rule requires the utmost diligence in those who are called to it. Men who judge that this special office is not needed neglect the importance of Christ's command for love among his disciples. They also neglect to see how the church often decays or is injured by ignorance of the duties. Ruling elders are required to preserve brotherly love in the church.

3. They are to encourage all the members of the church to fulfil their special church duties. There are duties required of each church member, according to their talents, whether spiritual or temporal. Some are rich, and some are poor. Some are young, and some are old. Some have peace, and some have trouble. Some have received more spiritual gifts and have more opportunity to use them. It is part of the rule of the church to admonish, instruct and exhort all to perform their duties. This is done not only publically in the preaching of the Word,

but also personally, as occasion requires. In particular, people are to be encouraged to contribute to the needs of the poor and to the church, according to the ability God in his providence has given them. Thus, there will be equality of giving in the church (2 Cor. 8:14).

4. They are to guard against the beginnings of any disorderly activity in the church. This includes watching out for those who fail to attend the meetings of the church (cf. Heb. 10:25). The very being and order of the church greatly depends on the constancy and diligence of the elders in this part of their work. Failure in this has often opened the door to all kinds of troubles and divisions. The result has been decay in faith, love and order to the dishonour of Christ and the danger of men's souls. First, one person stops regularly attending the meetings of the church. Then, another does so. Soon the whole lump is infected. If care is taken in this matter, it will result either in the healing and recovery of those who offend, or it will serve as a warning to others and keep the church from being corrupted or defiled (Heb. 3:12; 12:15).

5. They should visit the sick. This is especially the case if those who are sick are among the poor, the afflicted and those especially tempted. This is a general moral duty and a work of mercy, but it is also a church duty. If the officers of the church would diligently attend to this, it would not only give relief to needy people but would add much to the glory and beauty of our churches. I add

here, as a similar duty, that they should visit those who are imprisoned for their faith, whether for attending church meetings, or for fulfilling their duties as pastors or church officers. All the members of the church should do this if they have the opportunity but it is a particular responsibility of the elders. They represent the care and love of the whole church and even of Christ himself to his prisoners. The elders can then make known their needs to the entire church. The care of the early church in this matter was outstanding.

6. They are to advise and give direction to the deacons of the church in making provision for the poor of the church. While deacons are to serve the needs of people (see chapter 8), it is the task of the elders to inquire about the state of the poor, with all their circumstances. They are also to exhort the members to give generously towards these needs.

7. They are to keep funds that come from other churches in times of distress. The church might reach a state where the number of the poor is so multiplied among them that the church itself is not able to meet the needs of all. This might be due to suffering, persecution and affliction. If funds are sent to them out of love from other churches, the elders should keep these funds. They should then distribute them as they see fit (cf. Acts 11:30).

8. They should also consult with and inform the pastors and teaching elders concerning the state of the flock. This will be very useful for the pastors in directing their

ministry. If a pastor does not make it his business to know the state of the church in which he ministers in the Word and doctrine he fights uncertainly in the whole work. He is like a man beating the air. Given that pastors must give the greatest part of their time to the Word and prayer, they are given great assistance in knowing the whole flock when ruling elders share with them from their daily inspection, conversation and observation.

9. They are to meet and consult with the teaching elders about all the things that are to be proposed to the church. This provides a proper scrutiny of all proposals, avoids unnecessary conflicts and disputes, and helps preserve the authority of the elders.

10. They are to guard the proper liberties of the church that might be threatened by any self-important person, whether an officer or not.

11. They are to consult together with the other elders during times of difficulties and persecution. They are to consult about the present duties of the church and how to preserve it from violence, according to the will of Christ.

12. Given that there is often only one teaching elder, pastor, or teacher in a church, upon his death or removal, it is the duty of the ruling elders to preserve peace and unity in the church. This includes continuing the meetings of the church and giving direction and guidance for the church in the call and choice of a new pastor.

Many of the duties listed above are also generally required of all members. However, those who hold office have these as a special obligation. This should ensure that these duties are not neglected or that nothing is done in a confusing and disorderly way.

Conclusion

We have described here a beautiful order of things appointed by Christ in his church. When these officers exercise their distinct gifts the result is the edification of the church. When the church is lacking any of these it is bound to be defective to some extent. Where these defects are great the church lacks beauty, glory and order.

It is vain to believe that one teaching officer could attend with proper diligence to all the duties that belong to the rule of the church. No one man can have all these gifts in any eminent degree. Those who labour in Word and doctrine are to give themselves wholly to that task. They are to convince sceptics by word and writing, pleading for the truth. They are to give guidance and counsel and do many other things. A church may have a faithful pastor and greatly value his ministry but be unaware of the wisdom, goodness, love and care of Christ in instituting the office of ruling elder. Thus, the authority and benefit of proper government are in danger of being lost.

Those who rule are to do so diligently. No man alive can find anything lacking in this list for the church's edification. Neither can any man find anything listed here that is unnecessary or redundant. No sober man, knowing the care that these duties require, can suggest that they belong to only one and the same office, or that they can be done completely by one and the same person. In ancient times we have record of there being ten, twenty and even as many as forty elders in a particular church. In the Old Testament, they had a ruler for every ten families. In every church touched by reformation there should be some who attend to ruling who are not also called to labour in the Word and doctrine.

The purity, order, beauty and glory of the churches of Christ cannot be long preserved without a multiplication of elders in them. The number of elders should be in proportion to the number of their respective members. For lack of this, many churches have degenerated into anarchy and confusion, disputing and dividing into ruin. Others have given themselves over to some authoritarian teachers to rule them at their pleasure. This proved to be poison to the early churches. It will prove the same in the future if we neglect this order.

Some other views of church government

1. Some believe that the government of the church is absolutely democratic or popular. These judge that all church power or authority is in the community of the brethren, or body of the people. They look on elders or ministers as merely servants of the church. They believe that ministers or elders only have authority that is delegated to them by the church and not authority that comes directly from Christ. So, they sometimes appoint

persons who are not officers to administer the supper of the Lord or to lead in other solemn aspects of worship. Under this system, I see no need for elders at all and no direct necessity of any elders to rule.

2. Some place the government of many individual churches in the hands of a diocesan bishop. These are so far from understanding the need for many elders ruling in every particular church that they allow no effective rule by elders in them at all. However, a church without its own rulers is unknown to Scripture and early church history.

3. Others wrongly place the rule of individual churches in an association of all the elders from many churches acting together. In this system all acts of rule are done by many elders. This might be the best that some can do given their current circumstances. However, the need for there to be many elders in every particular church is the considered judgment and practice of the reformed churches in all places.

4. Some are beginning to maintain that an individual church needs only one pastor, bishop, or elder. These say that more than one elder for rule is unnecessary. This is a novel opinion. (1) It contradicts the practice of the church in all ages and in particular the pattern of the first churches constituted by the apostles (Acts 11:30; 14:23; 15:2,4,6,22; 16:4; 20:17; 1 Tim. 5:17; Phil. 1:1; Tit. 1:5; 1 Pet. 5:1). (2) Where there is only one elder in a church, there cannot be an eldership or a presbytery. It is like having a senate with only one senator and contradicts 1 Timothy

4:14. (3) The proper calling of officers is hindered if there is only one elder in every church, and he dies or is removed. The laying on of hands must then be left to the people or supplied by elders of other churches or wholly omitted. All of these options would be irregular. (4) When there is only one elder in a church it is difficult, if not impossible, to keep the rule of a church from becoming either overly centred in one man or decided merely by popular opinion. Where there is but one elder, extremes can hardly be avoided. If he rules by himself, without the advice and consent of the church, he becomes a dictator. If every matter must be considered by the whole church, the authority of the elder quickly becomes insignificant. He will be little more than any other brother in the society. These dangers are prevented by having many elders in each church. These can maintain the authority of the presbytery and free the church from the despotic rule of any Diotrephes who might arise (see 3 Jn. 9). (5) The very nature of the work of elders requires that in any church consisting of a considerable number of members that there must be more elders than one. In the Old Testament when God first appointed rule in the church he assigned that every ten persons or families be under a distinct ruler (Deut. 1:15). When elders watch over the walk and conduct of the members of the church it must be according to the rule of the gospel. Holiness is required. This requires great accuracy and circumspection in oversight. Elders must also give exact care and inspection to make sure that all church meetings are conducted in order and with decency. Only one who knows nothing about such things would think that one elder could do all this alone. Though a church without elders may have a good appearance for a season, if it does not comply with the wisdom of Christ, it has no lasting beauty and will not last for long.

Chapter 8
The office of deacon

Foundations

The distant foundations for the office of deacon lie in the
words of our Saviour: 'The poor always ye have with you' (Jn.
12:8). He both foretells that there will be poor in the church and
recommends care for them. He makes use of the words of the
law in Deuteronomy 15:11: 'The poor shall never cease out of the
land: therefore I command thee, saying, Thou shalt open thy
hand wide unto thy brother, to thy poor, and to thy needy.' The
Lord Christ by his own authority thus transfers and translates
this law for the use of gospel churches.

Provision for the poor was soon corrupted by hypocrisy
and greed. Judas complained that the ointment poured on our
Saviour might have been sold and the money given to the poor
but only because he was a thief and could take the money for
himself (Jn. 12:6). Judas began the murmuring but, according to
the gospel writers, at least some of the other disciples joined
him. In later ages, some clergymen, priests, friars and monks

became thieves, enriching themselves at the expense of those who were persuaded that they should give everything to the poor. In some cases, they took the greatest part of the wealth of a nation that professed the Christian religion.

Another foundation for this office was the preaching of the gospel among the poor. Many of those who first received the gospel were poor (Mt. 11:5; Jas. 2:5). So it was in the first ages of the church. This showed that the spread of the gospel was not by worldly schemes or for worldly advantage. God also declared in this how little he esteems the riches of this world. He was also giving the rich the opportunity to exercise grace by giving to the poor. This is the way that the rich can glorify God by their wealth. It would be good if all the churches and all their members would consider what an excellent duty it is to give to the poor. This is one of the highest duties of Christian societies. In this we exercise the spiritual grace of love.

The institution of the office of deacon

According to the institution of Christ, the first to have responsibility for the care of the poor were the church's first officers, the apostles. This is plain from the institution of the office of deacon in Acts 6:1-6. The whole work and care of the church was in the hands of the apostles. It was impossible, however, that they could handle everything. They gave themselves primarily to the more excellent and necessary work of preaching the Word and prayer. This was sufficient to fill all their time. Care for the poor was neglected, and resentment grew. Some began 'murmuring' about it. If the apostles had too much to handle, how is it that some men today think they can do everything in the church by themselves? In fact, they often do nothing in a proper manner. Whereas the apostles chose to give the priority to the work of prayer and preaching, many today lay aside this important work and apply themselves first to everything else!

The apostles certainly did not utterly abandon providing for the poor. Christ had given them this task from the beginning and they would not divest themselves of it. By the direction of the Holy Spirit, they provided the assistance needed for the work, so they would not be taken from their principal employment. Ordinary pastors and elders still have a duty to care for the poor. They should do this as long as it does not interfere with their principal work and duty. Of course, those who rightly understand these duties know they can spare little of their time and strength for much else.

The apostles, therefore, instituted the office of deacons. They did so by the authority of the Christ and the infallible guidance of the Holy Spirit. The deacons were to discharge this necessary and important duty which the apostles could not do themselves. Since the Lord Christ had committed the care of the poor to the disciples, there was now a declaration of his mind as to how this was to be done. This was a new office because the deacons were given a special work to do in the church; particular people were designated to do that work and they were given authority to do it.

Care for the poor

Three things are required to minister to the poor. First, there must be love and benevolence in the members of the church to contribute to this ministry. Second, there must be care and oversight for this ministry. Third, there must be the actual exercise and application of it. This final requirement is the particular task of the deacons. The love of the members for the poor is commanded by Christ and is a moral duty on everyone. Nobody should think that the appointment of deacons absolves him from his personal responsibility to act according to his own providential circumstances. The care for the whole work is the concern of the pastors and elders of the church, while the practical execution of this work is committed to the deacons.

The office of deacon was not a temporary institution but was intended to remain in the church through all generations: 'the poor ye shall have always with you'. There is a perpetual reason for its existence, because the pastors of the churches cannot do the whole work of praying and preaching and attend adequately to this ministry also. In addition, we see in the New Testament that deacons were among the regular officers of the church (see Phil. 1:1). They were not only in the church at Jerusalem, but also in the churches of the Gentiles. Direction is given for their continuation in the church, along with the qualifications needed by someone to be chosen and called to this office (1 Tim. 3:8-10;12-13). This includes the testing required if they are to be called to office (v. 10) and a promise of blessing for those who diligently serve in this office (v. 13).

The office of deacon is an office of service. Deacons are given no authority or power to rule in the church. They only have authority to complete their special work. This right is also confined to the particular churches to which they belong. They make their collections from the members of that church. They serve the members of that church. Extraordinary collections from or for other churches are to be made and overseen by the elders (cf. Acts 11:30).

The office of deacon was established to free the pastors of the churches from the care of outward things. Thus, it is the duty of the deacons not only to provide for the poor of the church but also to manage other affairs of the church of the same kind. This includes providing the place for church meetings. It includes providing the elements needed for the sacraments. It includes collecting, keeping and maintaining church property. It includes providing for the church's needs, especially in times of trouble or persecution. The deacons must pay attention to the needs of the elders at all times. They must make sure the church adequately provides for the elders. They must take directions from the elders. This was the practice of the early church until it was corrupted by greed and ambition.

Voluntary collections for the poor should normally be made every first day of the week (1 Cor. 16:1-2) but other collections can be made if necessary. The church's contributions should be given with generosity, not sparingly (2 Cor. 9:5-7). They should be given with equality, according to men's abilities (2 Cor. 8:13-14). They should be given proportionally. A portion is due to God 'as God hath prospered him' (1 Cor. 16:2). They should be given willingly and with freedom (2 Cor. 8:12). In fulfilling their office, the deacons should make known to the church the present needs of the poor. They should stir up the particular members to give, according to their ability. They should admonish those who neglect giving or who do not give in proportion to their ability. They should inform the elders of the church concerning those who persistently neglect their duty.

Deacons should also consider the state of the poor who receive contributions from the church. This too is part of their ministry. They should make sure that those receiving aid are poor indeed, and not merely pretending to be so. They should examine the degree of their poverty, including their relationships and circumstances, so they can receive suitable help. They should make sure that in other things they are walking according to the rule of the Christian life. In particular, they should make sure they are working and labouring according to their ability. Someone who is not willing to work should not eat at the expense of others. They should comfort, counsel and exhort them toward patience, submission, contentment with their condition, and thankfulness.

Qualifications of deacons

The qualifications of someone called to this office are distinctly laid down by the apostle Paul (1 Tim. 3:8-13). After a proper trial and assessment of their qualifications they are to be called to office. This call includes the choice of the church. It also includes separation to this office by prayer and the laying on of hands (Acts 6:3,5-6). We might add that to fulfil this office they must demonstrate mercy, to represent the tenderness of Christ toward the poor of the church (Rom. 12:8). They must demonstrate cheerfulness, so that care for the poor is not seen as being troublesome or burdensome to others. They must demonstrate diligence and faithfulness, so that they might enjoy the blessings promised in 1 Timothy 3:13.

Some final questions

It remains to ask a few questions about this office and those called to it:

1. Given that there are specific qualifications for the wives of those to be appointed as deacons (i.e., that they should be 'grave, not slanderers, sober, faithful in all things' [1 Tim. 3:11]), should a man continue in the office of deacon if his wife falls from the faith? My answer is that he who faithfully serves in this office might continue, even if his wife is removed by discipline from the church. Every one of us must give an account of himself to the Lord. He does not reject us for what we cannot remedy. The sinning person shall bear his own judgment. However, in such cases the deacon should do all he can to ensure that his wife gives as little offence as possible to the church.

2. May a deacon be dismissed from his office, after he has been set apart for it by prayer? In answer, we must remember that the purpose of the office is to serve the church. The continuation of men in the office must be regulated by the church. If the church at any time

does not need the ministry of this or that person, and it is his desire to step down, he may be removed from office. Men's outward circumstances may change so that they are not able to serve. In this case, they ought to be released. A man may be solemnly set apart by prayer for a work and duty for a limited season. It might, for example, only be for one year. When this season is over, he might then be dismissed from office. A deacon might also forfeit his office by unfaithfulness or other offences. If anyone leaves office due to contrariness, covetousness, laziness, or neglect it is a scandal and offence that the church should take notice of. The one who desires to be dismissed from office should therefore give an account of his reasons to the church. This way the ministry he held can be filled by the church, and a loving relationship can continue between him and the church.

3. How many deacons may there be in one congregation? There may be as many deacons as the church stands in need of to meet this ministry. The church can at any time increase the number of deacons as needed.

4. What is the duty of the deacons toward the elders of the church? The care of the whole church is principally committed to the pastors, teachers and ruling elders. The deacons are to inform the elders from time to time about the state of the church, especially concerning the poor. The deacons are to seek and take the advice of the elders in their work. They are also to assist the elders in all the outward concerns of the church.

5. May deacons preach the Word? The office of the deacon is instituted (Acts 6), and its qualifications are fixed (1 Tim. 3). It does not include a call to the ministry. In days of old, and today, some deacons might occasionally preach but they are not authorised to preach by virtue of being deacons.

Chapter 9
Church discipline

The power of the church towards its members may be described under three headings: (1) the admission of members into its society; (2) the rule and edification of those who belong to it; and (3) the exclusion of those who obstinately refuse to walk according to its laws and rules. The first of these was discussed in the opening chapters on how a church is formed. The second was discussed in the chapters on church offices and rule. We will now address the third heading, which is the power of excommunication.

Controversy and abuse

There has been a lot of debate on the subject of church discipline. As we shall see, however, nothing is more plain and simple. Nothing is more clearly instituted by Christ. Nothing is more wholesome or useful to the souls of men. However, it has been changed into a hideous monster by priestly dominion and tyranny. The Roman Catholic Church has used it to depose and assassinate kings and princes, to wage bloody wars, to bring terror to the souls of men, and to destroy their lives. They are ignorant of what true discipline is. If they would wake up, they would laugh at their folly. We need to be clear that the use of excommunication for temporal matters is completely contrary to what Christ has appointed.

These abuses have led some to an opposite extreme. They deny that excommunication was appointed or approved by the gospel. You cannot deny something, however, just because it has been abused. The best way to fight the corruption of church discipline is by returning to the original simplicity and purity of practice appointed by Christ and recorded in the Scriptures.

There has been great interest in the nature and exercise of excommunication in the Old Testament, but I intend primarily to consider what belongs to the churches under the New Testament.

The scope of discipline

1. All lawful societies are formed by voluntary agreement, according to the particular rules and laws of their own choosing. They have the right and power to receive members, to observe the rules of the society, and to expel those who wilfully deviate from those rules. Those who enter such societies should have the right and power to do so. Children, servants (employees) and subjects cannot be brought into membership in such societies by their parents, masters (employers), or ruler. The society's rules should be lawful, good and useful to the members and

others. The society must not oblige someone to neglect any duty that men owe to others. It must not bring hurt to its members. It should not require blind obedience to others. Finally, it must not promote things that are evil, sinful, superstitious, or idolatrous.

2. The power of a lawful society is confined only to those areas in which people may have benefits from that society. With churches, this means the power of expulsion is only in things that are spiritual. Churches are an institution of him whose kingdom is not of this world. The power of churches does not extend into the outward concerns of men, as to their lives, liberties, natural or political privileges, estates or possessions. Neglect of this principle led to abuses in the mediaeval Church of Rome. A poor man excommunicated by Rome lost his goods, liberty and life. By the law of the church and the land he was committed to jail. We need to be clear that the church cannot and must not control men's lives, liberties, houses and possessions. The privileges from which men are excluded in excommunication are not those of natural or civil rights but only those privileges that are granted to the church by Jesus Christ.

3. We also must acknowledge that every lawful society only has power over those who have joined it by their own accord. It has no power over outsiders. No one can be cast out who was never in! The apostle Paul makes that explicit in 1 Corinthians 5:12. A random power of

excommunication aimed at outsiders has no foundation in Scripture.

4. The only reason to expel a person from a society is a wilful deviation from the rules and laws of the society, which he consented to when he joined. The great rule of a church is that men do and observe what Christ commanded. None can be justly ejected from this society unless he wilfully disobeys Christ's commands. Men, therefore, cannot be cast out for light and trivial matters. To belong to a church a man must agree to walk in holy obedience to the commands of Christ, observing his institutions, without giving offence to others, and abiding in the truth. If he wilfully and obstinately transgresses in these things, it is the right and duty of the church, and in its power, to remove him from that society.

The authority of Jesus Christ for church discipline

The church has no power, except by the authority of Christ. Since excommunication is an act of authority we must demonstrate that church discipline was instituted by the express authority of Jesus Christ as implied by Paul's direction that excommunication be done 'in the name of our Lord Jesus Christ' (1 Cor. 5:4).

What is the scriptural evidence for excommunication as an express ordinance of our Lord Jesus Christ?

Firstly, this power is contained in the authority Christ gave to the church under the name of 'the keys of the kingdom of heaven'. This included not only doctrinal authority in preaching but also disciplinary authority. Christ designed his church to be holy, without blame, and without offence in the world. It represents his holiness and the holiness of his rule. Thus, he gave to the church the authority to cast out and separate from itself all who give offence by their sin. The neglect of discipline was a principal reason why the churches of the world for a long time lost their glory, honour and usefulness.

Secondly, discipline is directly instituted in Matthew 18:15-20: 'If thy brother shall trespass ... tell it unto the church: but if he neglect to hear the church, let him be unto thee as a heathen man and publican. Verily, I say unto you, Whatsoever ye shall bind on earth shall be bound in heaven: and whatsoever ye shall loose on earth shall be loosed in heaven.' The meaning should be plain. Trespasses are sins against God that bring scandal and offence. 'Church' refers to a particular Christian congregation. This church is to review the scandalous sins of its members, when they are brought before it in the proper manner described. It first seeks to recover the person from his sin by giving him counsel and advice. If he is obstinate, they are to remove him from fellowship. The rejection of an offending brother leaves him in the state of an unbeliever. He is declared liable to the displeasure of Christ and everlasting punishment, unless he repents. This is the excommunication we are advocating. This is the power that has been granted by Christ to the church.

Thirdly, we see discipline in the practice of the apostles. We have several instances:

1. We have the excommunication of Simon the magician, one who had professed faith and had been baptised. His wickedness convinced Peter that Simon had 'neither part nor lot' in the church (see Acts 8:13,20-23). It is true that this was the single act of one apostle, but it shows that the apostles were keen to preserve purity in the church.

2. We also have the discipline directed by the apostle Paul against the incestuous person in Corinth (1 Cor. 5:1-7). First, he declares the scandal of the sin (v. 1). Second, he blames the church for not acting to have the man 'taken away' or cut off from them (v. 2). Third, he declares his own judgment in the case, that this person ought to be removed (v. 3). Fourth, he declares the cause for this action: The Lord Jesus Christ has given this power to the church. The spirit of the apostle ('with my spirit') is there to give an authoritative declaration of judgment. It is done 'in the name of the Lord Jesus Christ, when ye are gathered together' (v. 4). Thus, they might 'purge out … the old leaven, that ye may be a new lump' (v. 7). The punishment is said to be 'inflicted by many' (2 Cor. 2:6). This means the whole church was involved (v. 7). They were also obliged to forgive him upon his repentance. The nature of the sentence is that he should be delivered to Satan 'for the destruction of the flesh, that the spirit may be saved in the day of the Lord Jesus' (1 Cor. 5:5). The whole of what we are pleading for is exemplified here.

There is a cause of excommunication, a scandalous sin and no repentance. There is preparation for its execution, the church's sense of sin and scandal and its humiliation. There is warrant for it in the institution of Christ and in the authority he has granted. There is a manner and form, an act of authority by consent of the whole church. There is a goal. For the church the goal is purging and vindication. For the person excommunicated, the goal is his repentance, reformation and salvation.

Some object that this was an extraordinary act by an apostle, but it is clear that it was the church that was given this authority and which exercised it in the rejection of the offender. There is nothing extraordinary in this case. Members of the church will fall into scandalous sin, and dishonour Christ and the church. It is an ordinary rule that the church should remove them unless there is repentance and reformation. Without this, the church cannot preserve its purity. Judgment was left to the church and Paul later commended them for it (2 Cor. 2:6-8).

Some have suggested that giving a man over to Satan (cf. 1 Tim. 1:19-20) was something only an apostle could do and that no such power is given to the church at present. However, this phrase does not mean to be physically tortured and killed, as some imagine. The purpose, rather, was the man's humiliation, recovery and salvation. This was the effect it actually had. The man was healed and restored. Delivery to Satan is no more than casting a man out of the visible kingdom of Christ with its privileges. It is giving him up, in his outward condition, into the state of the unbelievers who belong to the visible kingdom of Satan. Men are gathered into the church by conversion, the turning of them 'from the power of Satan unto God' (Acts 26:18). It is a delivery from the 'power of darkness' (the kingdom of Satan) and a translation into the kingdom of Christ (Col. 1:13). If a man rejects this, it is just to speak of him being re-delivered into the visible kingdom of Satan. If there is any spark of genuine grace left in him, the hope is that by shame, grief and fear he will be humbled. This passage, therefore, provides an everlasting rule given to the churches in all ages to preserve their purity.

3. In 2 Thessalonians 3:6 the apostle Paul gives commands to the brethren of the church 'in the name of our Lord Jesus Christ', to withdraw 'from every brother that walketh disorderly'. To 'walk disorderly' means to live in open disobedience to any of the commands of Christ. When he says, 'not after the tradition which he received of us', he means the doctrine of the gospel which he had delivered to them. This is a reference to the withdrawal of church fellowship. This cannot be done without some act of the church. If every member were left to his own judgment and practice the result would be confusion. Paul requires, therefore, that the church takes action (v. 14). He is to be denounced by a sentence against him

before fellowship is withdrawn. See also: Titus 3:10-11; 1
Timothy 5:20; and Revelation 2:2,14-15,20-21.

The role of the officers and the congregation

Some hold that there are two sorts of excommunication, one
'lesser' and the other 'greater'. Some have said there were three
sorts among the Jews. These degrees of excommunication are
not, however, found in the Scripture. The only excommunication
spoken of in the Bible is segregation from all participation in
church order, worship and privileges. Some hold that a person
should first be suspended from the Lord's Table for some time
before complete excommunication. This, however, is only an
act of prudence in church rule. No one should question that it
is sometimes the duty of church rulers to withhold the Lord's
Supper. If one refuses to submit to this, the church must
proceed to total removal of such a person from their whole
fellowship. The edification of the whole church must not be
obstructed by the disobedience of any one among them.

Excommunication is an act of church authority or rule. It
is done in the name of the Lord Jesus Christ. Since all rule is
in the hands of the elders, they are the ones who have power
of excommunication. The preservation of the purity of the
church, the vindication of its honour, the edification of all
its members, and the correction and salvation of offenders is
principally committed to them. They are best able to judge.
They have the best skill in the wisdom of spiritual rule.

Nevertheless, the interest and power of the whole church
must also be considered. When the apostle addresses discipline

he does not refer the matter only to the officers but to the whole church. This is evident in the places already cited.

1. The members of the whole church are to watch over one another. Each is to look out for the good, the honour, the reputation and the edification of the whole. Each also has a duty to purge out those who work against these ends. Those who are not concerned with these things are dead and useless members of the church. They must see that no root of bitterness springs up among them. They are not to be indifferent to defilement and scandal in their church. It is in their spiritual interest, as they take care of their souls, to agree in removing obstinate offenders.

2. There are some acts in the process of excommunication that the church must be involved in, or the whole process is rendered ineffective. The church must know the cause for the suggested discipline, or they cannot be blamed for neglect. They must be involved in the duties of preparation for discipline. This includes prayer, mourning and public admonition. They must also declare their consent by a common vote to exercise the power of the church.

3. The church also has duties toward a person who has been excommunicated. This includes praying for him. They must avoid fellowship with him, both public and private, that he may be ashamed. This comes from their voluntary acting in the exclusion. Without this, they will

feel no obligation and if they do not agree, the sentence is useless and invalid.

In conclusion, excommunication is an act of church power in both its officers and members. Officers and members must act according to the respective rights, interests and duties distinctively given to them. The officers act as officers, with authority, respecting the role of the congregation. The body of the church acts with power, respecting the role of the officers. Where either role is lacking, the whole duty is weakened, and church discipline becomes ineffectual.

The subjects of church discipline

Next, we need to look at those who are the objects of church discipline. Who ought to be excommunicated?

1. They must be members of that church which is excommunicating them. One church cannot excommunicate the members of another. They have no power to judge them. The foundation of the right to proceed against someone is the fact that they are voluntary members of the church.

2. They must obstinately continue in some scandalous sin, even after private and public admonition. The process for admonition in ordinary cases is given in Matthew 18:15-20. For a sin to be considered scandalous, it must be clearly judged to be so by all, without doubts, disputes, or hesitation. It must be a sin judged and condemned by the light of nature or by the express testimony of Scripture.

The Holy Spirit must bear witness that to continue in this sin without repentance is inconsistent with salvation. If it is dubious or disputable as to whether or not it is such a sin, there is no room for excommunication. If discipline is attempted in such cases it will become a matter of dispute, unsuitable to be agreed by the body of the church and liable to cause division. If limited to cases where scandalous sin is clearly recognised as inconsistent with salvation and persisted in, then the administration of excommunication will be plain and easy. Neglect of this rule has resulted in horrible confusion and disorder.

3. Before excommunication, the facts relating the sin to the offender must be either confessed, or not denied, or clearly proved. We will discuss some procedures later.

4. The biblical process of private and public admonition must have been followed. This requires patient waiting for the success of each of them. Patient admonition is necessary to convict the mind and conscience of the offender. It leaves him without either provocation against the church or excuse in himself. It expresses the grace and patience of Christ toward sinners. Omission of this will probably render the sentence useless and ineffectual.

5. The case must be judged and determined by the whole church in love and compassion. There are few so wicked who will not make some profession of sorrow and repentance, if the sin they are charged with is evident, and if it is justly proved against them. Such an expression

of sorrow might be sufficient to result in the church laying the process aside. This rule must be continually observed so that the least appearance of haste or undue process is avoided in all cases.

The manner of excommunication

How is excommunication to be administered according to the mind of Christ? The following are required:

1. There must be prayer. The administration of any solemn ordinance of the gospel without prayer horribly profanes it. The neglect of prayer or contempt for prayer by those who take it upon themselves to excommunicate others nullifies their actions. There must be due reverence for God and the solemn invocation of the name of Christ. When our Lord Jesus Christ gave his church the power of binding and loosing, he directed them to ask assistance by prayer when they gathered together (Mt. 18:18-20). The apostle Paul directs the church of Corinth to proceed with discipline when they gathered together (1 Cor. 5:4), and this must have included calling on the Lord's name. In brief, without prayer, excommunication is little more than a rash curse. Prayer should be offered in *preparation* for discipline. Prayer should be made for *guidance* in matters that are of such great weight and importance. It is no small thing to fall into mistakes when men act in the name of Christ or try to use his authority in ways he does not approve. The best of men and the

125

best of churches are liable to such mistakes when they are not guided by the Holy Spirit. This guidance is only received by prayer. Prayer should be offered in the *administration* of discipline. We should ask that what is done on earth will be ratified in heaven. We should pray that discipline will achieve its proper end. Prayer should be offered *after* discipline is administered. The church should join in praying for this same purpose. We should pray for the humiliation, repentance, healing and recovery of the offender.

2. There must be sadness. When Paul reproved the church of Corinth, he told them that they had not 'mourned' that the offender might be taken away from them (1 Cor. 5:2). In 2 Corinthians 12:21 Paul says that he will 'bewail' unrepentant sinners. There should be compassion for the person offending. He has cast himself into a dangerous condition. He is apart from the body. He is apart from worship. He is apart from the Lord's Table. His fall dishonours the gospel. No church should proceed to discipline until it is genuinely sad.

3. There must be a due sense of the future judgment of Christ. We judge for Christ in the matters of his house and kingdom. Woe to them who dare pronounce this sentence without being fully persuaded, on good grounds, that it is the sentence of Christ himself! It represents the future judgment, when Christ will eternally cut off from himself all hypocrites and unrepentant sinners. If we did this duty, we would keep ourselves from the corruptions that

many commit in exercising this power. This judgment must be corrective and not vindictive. It must be for healing and not for destruction. The church and all its members have a duty toward those who have been justly excommunicated. They are to pray for the person cut off, to admonish him as occasion allows, to show him compassion, to avoid common interactions, and to be ready for the restoration of love and all its fruits.

Eleven questions about church discipline

1. Should excommunication, though justly deserved, be omitted if it might bring the church into danger or trouble?

Troubles and dangers usually come in three areas: First, trouble might come from the act of discipline itself with respect to the law of the land. Second, trouble might come from the person being disciplined. He might be someone of great influence in the world. This might stir up persecution against the church. Third, trouble might come from lasting divisions created within the church.

To avoid troubles, the church and its officers must make sure they do not act sinfully and give occasion to these dangers. The cause for excommunication must be clear and evident. The merits of the case and the process of applying discipline must be so clear that no rational, unbiased observer would object to this action. This must be true of all cases of church discipline. Sufficient space and time must be given for repentance and for giving the church opportunity to admonish the person. The church must also show that it really suffers in its honour and reputation by tolerating such a scandalous offender among them.

If these things are properly done, the church has no reason to overlook the exercise of discipline. First, the church's actions should not touch on human laws. Church discipline does not touch men's lives, liberties, estates, or secular privileges. The law of the land should no more be involved than when a parent disinherits a rebellious child. Second, the church should not fear persecution that comes from discipline of any person. If we use this excuse we will never obey Christ. The apostles were not afraid to practise discipline against Simon Magus, Hymeneus and Alexander, and others. The Lord commends or reproves his churches for faithfulness in this area (see Rev. chapters 2-3). He will take care of his church and turn all things for their advantage. Third, as for divisions in the church, proper rule, order, love and duty will prevent such differences. Those who fail to follow Christ's appointed process in discipline bear their own blame for creating such divisions.

2. What if an offender, who justly deserves to come under discipline, voluntarily withdraws from or leaves the fellowship of the church? Is it necessary to proceed with excommunication against him?

Some say it is enough to declare in the church that this person has cut himself off from the fellowship of the church. Thus, he is no longer under their watch or care and is left to himself in the world. However, I believe that it undermines the authority of the church.

Again, the case must be clear. The offence must be plain, open, scandalous and persisted in. The admonition of the church must have been despised and not complied with. Then, it is the duty of the church to excommunicate him despite his voluntary departure. No man can free himself from the church's censure simply by voluntary removal. It is necessary for the church to do its duty and to vindicate its honour. It will benefit in edification from the duties of humiliation, mourning and prayer that are necessary for carrying out this discipline. It is also necessary for the good and benefit of the person deserving to be excommunicated. The goal of discipline is his correction, not his destruction. It seeks his repentance and recovery. It is to be followed with sharp admonition and prayer in hopes that in due time this will reach even the most hardened sinner. The wisdom and order of the church must be respected. We must also remember that the authority to exercise discipline is given to the church so that it might give a testimony of the future judgment of Christ against unrepentant sinners. No one can run away from or escape this judgment!

3. In a case of great and scandalous sin, may a church proceed to excommunication without previous admonition?

We must remember that men may be falsely accused of the greatest sins as well as lesser ones. These false accusations may come in particular testimonies and in public reports.

This happened to the Lord Jesus Christ himself! Therefore, all hasty and precipitous actions are to be carefully avoided even when the claim is pressed that the sin is great and notorious. David, for example, was too hasty in judging the case of Mephibosheth. The actual sins of individuals must be understood in their circumstances. The church is to make careful inquiry and obtain full knowledge. These things must be duly weighed with a godly attitude. This is essential to the right administration of discipline. Discipline against a person cannot take place without personal conference with the individual. He must be allowed to speak for himself. If guilt is discovered, this conference is a form of admonition in the disciplinary process.

4. In cases where the sin is great and notorious should the church proceed to excommunication even if the person repents and expresses humiliation to the satisfaction of the church?

In an orderly disciplinary process regarding private sins, if repentance comes in the first or second admonition then this ends the process of church discipline. What if the sin is great and harms the church reputation? I still say that if the rulers of the church are convinced that the repentance is sincere, the church cannot proceed with excommunication against the offender. If they do proceed, they are publically rejecting someone who Christ receives. To do this is to set themselves up against Christ. It is to use his authority against his mind and will. Such a sentence destroys itself. It declares that Christ does not approve someone he does approve. This would be a misrepresentation of the gospel and of the Lord Christ. The gospel says that all sinners who repent will be pardoned and accepted. The rejection of someone who has truly repented contradicts this. This is dangerous to the faith of believers, especially with regard to doctrine. To discipline one whom Christ has accepted makes the church a teacher of lies. Such action is also contrary to the nature and goal of discipline. The sole end of church discipline is the humiliation, repentance and recovery of the sinner. If this is gained, then it is contradictory for discipline to continue. Some will say that church discipline also has the goal of preserving the church's purity and protecting its honour and reputation from scandalous sins. I respond that no church can be made impure by including those whom Christ has purged. It is no dishonour for a church to have sinners in it who have sincerely repented. If needed, while the offence and scandal is still fresh, the church can prudentially require the offending person to abstain from the Lord's Table for a season.

5. Should a member be excommunicated who leaves the fellowship of a church voluntarily, without a cause, but in a disorderly manner?

The goal of all particular churches is the edification of their members. A person may justly move from the fellowship of one church to another in order to care for his own edification. No church should deny such a person his liberty, when it is peaceably done. Suppose a person desires to depart from a particular congregation. He is free from scandalous sin. He departs quietly, without creating disorder or confusion in the church. Then, he actually joins himself to the fellowship of another church, whose order, principles and worship are approved. In this case, the church should not attempt to exercise discipline. It is enough to declare that this person, of his own accord, has left the fellowship of the church and is no longer under its watch and care. The church is no longer especially obligated to him, beyond general Christian duties. If the departure is accompanied by other evils, the situation is quite different. If there are complaints and false accusations (as is often the case), they may need to proceed with church discipline.

6. How much time should be allowed, after admonition is given, before proceeding to actual excommunication?

The nature of church discipline requires a considerable space of time between solemn admonition and excommunication. This is so, because the goal of discipline is the repentance and recovery of the offender. This will only come gradually. Lack of light and exasperation may seem to frustrate the admonition. However, if they will only suspend the process, it may afterwards affect the conscience of the offender. Since it is an admonition coming from the church, the church has the duty to abide in prayer and waiting for the fruit of its admonition, according to the appointment of Christ. This may require that a long period of time be spent in waiting.

No present appearance of obstinacy or lack of repentance under admonition should cause an immediate move toward excommunication. This would not represent the patience and forbearance of Christ toward his church, and all its members. It does not fit the rule of love which 'hopeth all things, beareth all things' etc. All grounds of hope for the recovery of sinners by repentance are to be given attention, so as to defer the ultimate sentence. If the offender adds new sins, of the same kind or any other, while under admonition, it indicates that the discipline should proceed.

7. Should a man be excommunicated for errors in matters of faith or for false opinions?

The answer is plainly and positively stated in Scripture (see Rev. 2:2,6,14,15,20; 1 Tim. 1:19-20; Tit. 3:10-11, and other places).

If the errors concern the fundamental truths of the gospel, the church is to cut off those who hold those views from their fellowship. Those affirming such errors make 'shipwreck of the faith'. We cannot ignore the problem, because we like the person or we want to keep the peace. This evil is a danger to the whole church. It is like gangrene. A church is without excuse which omits this duty.

False opinions in lesser things may be tolerated in a church. These do not immediately concern the foundation of faith and Christian practice. Various rules are provided in Scripture (e.g., Rom. 14:1-3, ff.; Phil. 3:15-16). In general, it is best for their edification if believers peaceably join churches with which they most closely agree on such principles and opinions, especially with regard to the duties of worship.

8. If a person is excommunicated from a church, may he be allowed to attend the public preaching services of that church?

This may be permitted, just as the heathens and unbelievers attend worship (1 Cor. 14:23-24). When people are under a church's discipline, the church is hopeful of their recovery and return. It does not, therefore, want to prohibit them from receiving the preaching of the Word.

9. How are we to understand the rules given by the apostle towards those who are rejected by the church (e.g., 1 Cor. 5:11: 'with such an one no not to eat'; 2 Thess. 3:14: 'Note that man, and have no company with him, that he may be ashamed')?

To 'eat' includes all the ordinary interactions in the things of this life. This rule forbids interactions by choice with the one excommunicated. This includes conversation about earthly, secular things but it does not forbid spiritual conversations. He ought still to be admonished, while he will hear words of admonition. It does not affect necessary business transactions. It also does not suspend the natural and moral duties of relationships, such as those between a husband and wife, parents and children, magistrates and citizens, masters (employers) and servants (employees), neighbours, and among family members. Husbands may not forsake their wives, if they are excommunicated, nor wives their husbands. Magistrates may not withdraw protection from their citizens, because they are excommunicated. Citizens, likewise, may not withhold obedience to magistrates. The same is true in all other natural and moral relationships.

The purpose of prohibiting ordinary interactions with those under discipline is to show our condemnation of the sin and our disapproval of the one guilty of it. It also keeps us from participating in his sin. It should make him ashamed of himself. The hope is that if he is not given up to total apostasy, this will cause him to think of returning.

10. How should people who were excommunicated by the church be received if they repent?

They should be received with all readiness and cheerfulness. They should be received with meekness, to take away any discouragement (Gal. 6:1). They should be received with compassion, consolation and love (2 Cor. 2:7-8). They should be received with joy, representing the heart of Christ toward repenting sinners.

Outwardly, they should give a testimony of their repentance that satisfies the church, and the church should give its consent to their reception. They should again affirm the church covenant and become members. The elders should go before the church to present this.

We must beware of being too hard towards those excommunicated. Some will not re-admit lapsed sinners even after they repent. Even worse, some do not seek the recovery of those they have excommunicated. They do not pray for them, admonish them, and exhort them. They do not have a meek and tender spirit. They are glad that they have gone. It is better never to excommunicate anybody, than it is to act in this way toward those who are excommunicated.

11. Can excommunication ever be regular and valid when the rightness of the matter is dubious and disputed?

This is the situation with many matters of life and personal interactions. It is also the case when a fact is not proved by positive witnesses on the one hand, and it is denied on the other.

The effectiveness of excommunication depends on the conviction of the consciences of the people that are to be excommunicated. If they have no sense of guilt, as in dubious cases, the sentence will have no force or effectiveness. If good and wise men have a difference in judgment, then it is a dubious case. There should be no censure. Nothing should be done unless it is clearly agreed by the judgment of those that fear God. If the case relates to a right or wrong in something involving civil law the church is no judge in such cases.

If the question is about doctrines that are not on fundamental points and those who dispute with the church do so peaceably and orderly, there is no need for discipline. If they insist on their opinions, wrangle and contend over them, and break the peace of the church, however, there are rules for that.

If the establishment of facts requires witnesses, it is absolutely necessary that there be two or three witnesses. Only one witness will not be sufficient (see Deut. 19:15; Num. 35:30; Mt. 18:16, etc.).

Basic rules for excommunication

Here is a summary of the basic rules to be regarded in excommunication:

1. No excommunication is to be allowed in dubious and disputable cases. This includes cases where right and wrong are not easily determined by an unprejudiced person who knows the will of God in such things. This includes cases that require testimony and there are not at least two witnesses.

2. All prejudices, all partiality, all provocations, and all hastiness are to be carefully avoided in this process. The judgment is the Lord's.

3. In the process of church discipline we are to charge our consciences with the mind of Christ, asking what he would do. We are to consider the love, grace, mercy and patience that he showed when coming down into this world.

4. We must constantly remember that we too are in the flesh and are liable to temptation. This will restrain the forwardness and confidence that some are prone to manifest in such cases. In all these things a watchful eye is to be kept over Satan. He always seeks to pervert discipline into the destruction of men and not their edification. He too often succeeds in this. If the church is negligent in the management and pursuit of discipline and Satan perverts it to the ruin of any, it is the fault of

the church, because they have not been careful of the honour of Christ.

Final remarks

1. Superstitious Roman Catholic practices of excommunication with the noise and clamour of a bell, a book, or a candle are to be rejected.

2. It is a misrepresentation of Christ and his authority for people who are openly guilty of profane sin to excommunicate those who are blameless in all matters of Christian obedience.

3. Excommunication cannot be valid if it seeks to oppose the gospel or is done in a manner that contradicts the gospel.

4. Despite all the arguments and confusion caused by false practices, we insist that the smallest number of sincere Christians in any church may (and should) exercise proper church discipline to the glory of Christ and to their own edification.

Chapter 10
Fellowship among churches

Churches ought to have fellowship with each other. The goal of each particular church is the edification of the body of Christ in general, the universal church. As they promote the edification of the universal church, they promote their own edification, since they are parts and members of it.

All churches, from the beginning, were in need of help in preserving the truth. The Lord Jesus Christ committed the care of the churches to the apostles during their lives. Paul calls this 'the care of all the churches' (2 Cor. 11:28). After the death of the apostles, our Lord appointed fellowship among particular churches to edify the church universal in faith, love and peace. Each church has been given gifts and graces to edify the whole.

In this fellowship, all churches are equal. Wherever there is a church, whether in a city or a village, they share equally in this fellowship. Of course, some churches have advantages over others. Some might become more useful and helpful than others but none of them is subordinate to another. Abuse of these advantages is what destroyed church fellowship, as the church at Rome began to have authority over other churches.

While each church essentially has equal fellowship with all other churches in the world, the actual exercise of this fellowship will normally be more limited to those that are nearby or which have providentially been brought into contact. Yet the world is not so wide that we cannot speak of a fellowship among all churches, 'from the rising of the sun, even to the going down of the same'. No true church is or can be excluded from this fellowship.

Roman Catholic error

In the Roman Catholic Church, the pope is seen as the head and centre of all church union. No churches can have union with Christ or with each other except through the pope. If anyone does not submit to the pope he is considered by them to be a stranger and foreigner to the church universal. This hierarchy sets the pope up as Antichrist, in direct opposition to Christ as the head of the church (cf. Eph. 4:15-16; Col. 2:19). The suggestion that there can be a twofold head of the universal church, Christ the invisible head and the pope the visible head, is completely foreign to Scripture. It was unknown in the first six hundred years of church history. The Roman system sets up an antichristian church state in opposition to Christ and the true universal church.

Episcopal error

There are also those who claim to have fellowship not under the pope but under diocesan bishops. This system, however, is also destructive of the church and its fellowship. It limits the fellowship of a church to a province or nation. It also makes a particular local church subject to officers that are not members of that church. This arrangement cannot be found in Scripture and so did not arise by divine institution, neither was it the practice in the early years of church history.

True union

Particular churches are in union because they all have one and the same God and Father, one Lord Jesus Christ, one faith and one doctrine of faith, one hope of their calling, one regeneration, one baptism, one bread and wine, and are united in one Spirit through the bond of faith and love. Two things complete the union of churches:

1. *Their union with Christ.* Christ is the origin and spring of this union. Every particular church is united to him as its head. Besides him, it has no head. The apostle Paul affirmed Christ as the head of the church (Eph. 4:15-16; Col. 2:19). Each church is also in God the Father, or has God as its Father (2 Thes. 1:1). Unless a church is disunited from Christ it cannot be disunited from the universal church. This bond springs from Christ and is the work of the Holy Spirit acting in them by faith and love. This is the kingly, royal, beautiful union of the church. Christ, as the only head of influence and rule, brings it into relation to himself as his body. He communicates his Spirit to it. He governs it by the law of his Word. He enables it to obey the duties of faith, love and holiness. He makes it

observe his commands for divine worship. This spiritual relationship gives the church its reality and power which is then demonstrated by its outward activities.

2. *Their union with each other.* The churches relate to each other as equals. Their bond is the special love that Christ requires among all his disciples. There may be failures in some of them. There may be differences among them. But while the substance of them is preserved, the union of all churches is preserved. This is the blessed oneness which the Lord Christ prayed for so earnestly (Jn. 17:20-23).

The union of all particular churches as the universal church is always the same. It does not change. It includes all the churches in the world at all times. It cannot be confined to a single country or denomination. The gates of hell cannot prevail against it. All challenges to its union are in direct opposition to the prayers and promises of Jesus Christ. While evangelical faith, holiness, obedience to the commands of Christ, and mutual love abide in any churches on the earth, there is a universal church.

What is the fellowship of churches?

The fellowship of churches is their joint actions in the same gospel duties toward God in Christ. This includes their mutual actions toward each other as they fulfil their purpose of glorifying Christ and edifying the whole universal church. The ground for this fellowship is faith. This is the first act of the fellowship of churches. There are five ways in which churches then share in fellowship:

1. In general, they believe the same doctrine of truth. They hold the same articles of faith and make the same public profession. Every one of them is the pillar and ground of the truth. The early church provided for this in creeds or confessions of faith. In time this came to be abused. The Arians produced as many creeds as the orthodox. For the fellowship of all particular churches in the world, nothing is required but belief of the Scripture to be the Word of God, provided that no error is promoted that is contrary to the principal and fundamental doctrines of Scripture. Although a group of people might profess the Scripture to be the Word of God, they would cut themselves off from fellowship with the universal church if they embraced serious error. Such errors would include denial of the holy Trinity, of the incarnation of the Son of God, of his divine person or office, of the redemption of the church by his blood, of the necessity of regeneration by his Spirit, and the like. They also might add things that would exclude them from fellowship with the universal church. This would include holding their traditions as equal with the written Word, saying there is another head of the church besides the Lord Jesus Christ, saying there are other sacrifices needed other than what Christ offered once for all, and the like. But where any have been preserved from these kinds of heresies, no more

is required for fellowship with the whole church but the kind of belief described above.

2. They also believe in the church itself. This fellowship requires the belief that the Lord Christ has had in all ages a church on the earth that cannot be confined to particular places or human organizations. This church is redeemed, called and sanctified by him. It is his kingdom, his interest, his concern in the world. All the promises of God belong to this church and its members. He will save, deliver and preserve this church from all opposition. After death, he will raise it up and glorify it at the last day. This is the faith of the universal church in itself. It is an ancient, fundamental article of our religion. If anyone denies that there is such a church he cuts himself off from the fellowship of the church of Christ.

3. They pray. The fellowship of churches in faith consists to a large extent in the principal fruit of that faith, namely, prayer. So, in Ephesians 2:18, it says that through Christ we 'have access by one Spirit unto the Father'. Paul continues the emphasis on fellowship in vv. 19-22. Prayers in all churches have one object. They are directed to God as Father. They proceed from one and the same Spirit. A Spirit of grace and supplication is given to them to make intercession for them. All is continually offered to God by the same High Priest. He adds to it the incense of his own intercession. By him they have all access to the same throne of grace. They have a blessed fellowship in prayer continually. This fellowship is more

evident in that the prayers of all are for all. There is not a single particular church or a single member of any of them that does not have the prayer support of all the churches in the world and all the members of them every day. Although this fellowship is invisible to the eyes of flesh, it is glorious to the eye of faith. It is a part of the glory of Christ, the mediator in heaven. This fellowship in prayer gives to all churches a communion far more glorious than any outward rite or plan of men's devising. If there are any people or churches who pray to anyone other than God the Father, or who rely on any mediator other than Christ alone, or who renounce the aid of the Holy Spirit, they cut themselves off from fellowship with the universal church.

4. They administer the same sacraments of baptism and the Lord's Supper. These are the same in, to, and among them all. Variations in the outward manner of their administration do not interrupt that fellowship. Wherever the continuation of these ordinances is denied, fellowship with the universal church is broken. It is also broken if the nature and use of these ordinances is perverted, or if idolatrous worship is added to their administration.

5. They profess that they are subject to the authority of Christ in all things. This means that they are under obligation to do and observe all that Christ has commanded.

Other points might be added, but these five are sufficient to show the real, evangelical fellowship shared among churches.

The bond of love

The bond of this union is love. This is not the common love that men have for their fellow men. It is a special grace of the Holy Spirit, acting in the church and so was called 'a new commandment' by Christ. The Holy Spirit of grace and love is given from Christ, the fountain and centre of all church union. The Holy Spirit dwells in and abides in his church and so the church is united to Christ. The Holy Spirit works a mutual love in the church and all its members. This moves them to engage in mutual acts of love toward one another as members of the same body. This is the union every church has within itself. It is also the union that all churches have among themselves. This kind of union and fellowship among churches may seem strange to those who look to outward rules, rites and ceremonies for these things. The church, however, is dependent on Christ for its edification. This love works effectively in every office, officer and member, giving the whole both its union and fellowship. All the church's actions are guided by divine rule.

Some want to make the church like a machine, held together by the iron joints and bands of human laws. They act with weapons that are not spiritual but carnal. They cast the members of the church into a prison of outward conformity. Thus, they forsake the Scripture and follow their own imagination.

Synods or Councils

The outward acts of fellowship, proceeding from this love consist of advice and assistance. Churches have outward fellowship in synods or councils. Synods are the meetings of various churches by their messengers or delegates to consult about and determine matters of common concern.

The need and warrant for such synods is clear first by the light of nature. All societies that have the same origin, rule, interest and purpose will have a natural concern for each other. Churches are such societies. When a difficulty arises in one of them that cannot be overcome it is reasonable to think that advice and counsel is needed.

Such synods are also justified by the fact that all churches are brought under one Head, by one Spirit, through one faith and worship to the same ends. All churches therefore form one mystical body. None of them can be absolutely complete without acting with other members of the same mystical body for the common good of the whole, as occasion requires. Any joint action must be by general discussion and agreement. This can only happen if messengers and delegates come together in synods. As in the early church, some problems might be dealt with by one church writing a letter to another seeking advice and counsel but many cases cannot be reconciled or determined unless there is an actual conference (see Acts 15). No church is so independent that it can always determine its duties to the Lord Christ and the universal church on its own, without consulting with others. The church that keeps all such matters within its own assemblies cuts itself off from fellowship with the universal church. No man can safely commit his soul to such a church.

Synods were instituted by Jesus Christ. This institution did not come by direct command. It is evident by the nature of the church itself. The institution of synods is also supported by the example of the apostles. Christ built his churches to have mutual relations with each other. None of them can be complete or fulfil their whole duty without mutual advice and counsel with other churches. Thus, Christ ordained that they have fellowship in synods. Christ himself is present in such meetings.

The goal of all particular churches is the edification of the church universal, to the glory of God in Christ. This goal will be sinfully neglected without synods. Truth, peace and love may be lost among churches. The union of the universal church in them may be dissolved if there is not a way to preserve and repair it. The particular church that does not extend its duty beyond its own meetings and members misses its principal goal. Every principle, opinion, or persuasion that leads a church to confine its care and duty to its own edification, neglecting the edification of the church universal, is schismatic. This is also true if the church only has fellowship with those churches that agree with it in some particular practice.

There is an order and method of church discipline given by Christ himself in Matthew 18:15-17. The final part of this process is taking it to the church. There is no doubt that the church has the power to retain or reject an offender. This is necessary to preserve the church's outward order and peace.

But no church is absolutely infallible in its judgment in every case. The church's action may be so doubtful that it does not affect the conscience of the person censured. Such a person is not only a member of that particular church, but he is also a member of the universal church. It is necessary, therefore, that his interests be heard and judged, if he desires it. This can only be done by the kinds of synods or councils that we have described.

Synods are consecrated for use by the church in all ages by the example of the apostles in guiding the first churches of Jews and Gentiles (Acts 15).

Matters for Synods to consider

Synods should consider anything that disturbs the fellowship of churches. Here are some examples:

1. Matters of faith. Churches are to have fellowship in the profession of the same faith. If doubts or differences arise in any particular church or among various churches, the last outward means for preserving the rule of faith would be for synods or councils to meet in order to condemn the error. Care for right doctrine is first committed to each local church. In some cases, however, a church may not be able to rebuke or suppress a person who is teaching false doctrines. Other churches might be in danger of being infected or defiled. A synod or council is then the last external refuge to preserve the fellowship

of churches in the same faith. We have many examples of this in the early church before it degenerated.

2. Matters of peace, order and unity. Every particular church ought to enjoy order, peace and unity among its own members. There were schisms, divisions, arguments and contentions, however, even among the churches planted and watered by the apostles (e.g., at Antioch, Corinth and in some of the churches of Galatia)! The duty of remedying and healing these divisions and differences, whatever their cause, first rests with each particular member in every such church. If every one of them did their duty in love this would put an end to all strife. If individuals fail, the whole church has the responsibility to rebuke and reconcile such differences. In cases where the church is not able to do this, the last outward means to seek reconciliation is an assembly of other churches walking in actual fellowship with that church. This is what happened in the church at Antioch (Acts 15).

3. Matters of improper use of church discipline. Synods are needed when any members have been injured by maladministration of discipline. Some might be unduly cast out of the church by the power and interests of some Diotrephes. Some members of the church might make a party or faction to depose their elders. In cases like this, it is necessary both for the fellowship of the churches and the interest of the persons who have been injured that the proceedings of such a church be reviewed by a synod and remedy be provided. It was not the mind of

the apostles that they should be left without relief who are unduly cast out of the church by any Diotrephes. There is no ordinary way to provide this but by synods.

4. Matters of worship. Credible news may come that a church has introduced superstition or vanity into its worship. The members of a church might walk in the manner described by Paul in Philippians 3:18-19. This dishonours the gospel and the ways of Christ, but the church is not calling for repentance and reformation. Other churches that have fellowship with that church ought to have a synod for advice. They might suggest ways to address this problem to that church's elders. If the church is obstinate in its evil ways, they might decide to withhold fellowship from that church. Lack of attention to the purity of gospel worship and gospel obedience in the fellowship of churches has led to decay and apostasy among all. By neglecting this matter, the churches fail to be helpful to one another in their mutual recovery and revival of things that are ready to die. Instead, they gradually infect one another.

Considering what we have learned by the woeful experience of churches in later ages that have degenerated in gospel worship and holiness, it would not be wrong to suggest that like-minded churches meet frequently in synods. In these meetings they can inquire into the spiritual state of them all. They can give advice for correcting things that are amiss. They can preserve the purity of worship and the proper exercise of discipline. They can especially demonstrate the power and fruit of evangelical obedience.

Thus we see the goal of such synods among the churches of Christ. Their general goal is to promote the edification of the whole body or universal church. They are to prevent divisions over differences in judgments and practices. The first Christian synod was an assembly of the first two churches in the world by their delegates. The first church of the Jews was at Jerusalem. The first church of the Gentiles was at Antioch. The first synod was arranged to prevent divisions and to preserve fellowship between them (Acts 15). Synods are to meet to avoid or cure offences against mutual love. They are to advance the light of the gospel by a joint confession and agreement in the faith. They are to give joint testimony against wicked heresies or errors that have overthrown or threaten to overthrow the faith of any. They are to offer relief to any who have been unfairly cast out of a church by any Diotrephes.

The extent of Synods

What should the extent of a synod be? It is impossible to have a council that includes the whole church of Christ on earth with representation of all particular churches. Such councils never were and probably never will be able to meet, and they are not, in fact, needed for the edification of the church.

Synods should be arranged on the basis of convenience. Some churches will be better able to promote edification than others. Such was the case when the church at Jerusalem was able to assist the church at Antioch. Some churches are planted so far from each other that it would be impossible for them to have their messengers meet together. In some cases a church cannot meet because of difficulties and dangers. Sometimes churches in different countries would find it hard to overcome their national interests. The so-called 'ecumenical councils' of the Early Church never really extended beyond the Roman Empire. Spiritual prudence is therefore needed so that churches gather in synods in ways that are safe and convenient and with the particular churches that will be appropriate for the purpose.

Who attends Synods?

Synods should consist of people chosen and delegated by their respective churches for the purpose. This is consistent with the example of Scripture and common sense. So it was in the first example of such a meeting (Acts 15). The church at Antioch chose and sent messengers from their own number to consult with the apostles and elders of the church at Jerusalem. The members of that church were also present. This was also the practice in the first three hundred years of the church. Only later was the whole nature of church synods lost and buried, and true religion almost destroyed.

The elders or officers of the churches, or at least some of them, should be the chief delegates and messengers. They have particular care for public edification. They are rightly presumed to know best the state of their own churches. They are best able to judge the matters under consideration. They better represent the churches from whom they are sent than any private brethren can do. They receive the respect and reverence which is due to the churches themselves. They are also the most capable of recommending the decisions of the synod to their churches. A contrary practice would quickly introduce confusion.

The calling of Synods

Synods can only be called by the voluntary consent of the churches who desire to meet together by their delegates or messengers. A government official might invite bishops, pastors, or ministers, along with others to give him advice about the concerns of religion and the church in the region under his authority. There have been some occasions where this has been beneficial, but it is not the same as a synod.

Church synods should not be concerned with civil affairs. This is beyond their jurisdiction. They can only make decisions relating to the doctrines and practices of the churches. They should seek to meet in outward peace by the permission of the civil authorities, but if they cannot obtain this permission, they must do what Christ's law requires.

The power and authority of Synods

Synods have a threefold power. They can *declare* the mind of God in Scripture by authoritative teaching. They can *appoint* things to be believed or practised. They can *act* towards people or churches. These decisions may affect those churches that send representatives and take part in the discussions but might also relate to someone being censured or excommunicated, or to a church that had acted in a disorderly way towards others.

A church should accept the findings and decrees of a synod if it is convinced by the scriptural reasons given. When declaring the mind of Christ from the Scripture relating to doctrine, or giving advice about practice, a synod is acting in harmony with both the mind of Christ and the example given by the apostles (Acts 15). Christ is present with his people, and they are acting with his authority, to which all should submit. In other cases, a church may submit for the sake of conscience, recognising the authority of the synod itself.

After a synod, the churches should therefore humbly consider the evidence to determine whether Christ was present. They can discern this partly by the manner, cause, goal and conduct of the entire meeting. They also need to assess how the outcome relates to the Word of God and whether the Scriptures were given their rightful pre-eminence so that the decisions made were drawn from its truth and confirmed by its authority.

Unless such judgment is exercised, no one is bound by the decisions of synods. There have been many assemblies of bishops with the outward appearance and title of synods or councils, but they were really dens of thieves, robbers and idolaters. The affairs of such synods were handled with wrath, horrible craftiness and for selfish interest, to the ruin of the church. When the church is declining in faith, worship and holiness, nothing is to be more feared than such synods! They can open a door for all kinds of errors and superstitions to enter the church. The idea that synods have absolute authority to issue orders and decrees that must be obeyed under the penalty of excommunication and that they have jurisdiction over churches or individuals is a human invention. It comes from the fourth century of the church, when the progress of fatal apostasy became visible.

The Jerusalem Council

In concluding, it will be useful to note some things about the Jerusalem Council, as recorded in Acts 15:

1. The occasion of the council was a dispute in the church at Antioch. They could not settle this among themselves, because those who caused the difference pretended to have authority from the apostles (vv. 1,24).

2. The meeting took place because of the voluntary desire of the church at Antioch to refer the matter to the church at Jerusalem. Their mutual fellowship was at risk and therefore they sent their messengers for consultation.

3. The synod comprised the apostles, elders and brethren of the church of Jerusalem, along with the messengers from Antioch, including Paul and Barnabas.

4. The matter of dispute was debated, searching for the mind of God concerning it, in the Scripture, and out of the Scripture. The final decision came from James' proposal.

5. Nothing new was imposed upon the churches. They were simply reminded that Gentile converts must

abstain from fornication and from using their liberty in such a way as to provoke scandal. This was the duty of all Christians even before the decision was made.

6. The synod proposed acceptance of its decree on the grounds that it was the mind of the Holy Spirit (v. 28). They may have known this by immediate revelation but most likely because it was written or recorded in Scripture. We can conclude that nothing is to be proposed or confirmed in synods but what is well known to the Holy Spirit in Scripture, either by immediate revelation or by Scripture revelation. These grounds included the authority of the assembly convened in the name of Christ and by virtue of his presence: 'It seemed good to the Holy Ghost, and to us'. It also included the fact that this decision was 'necessary' to avoid scandal. Finally, it included the duty of peace and mutual fellowship between the Jewish and Gentile churches. The way in which they explained their decree shows that their authority was doctrinal.

7. They described their decree limiting the liberty of Gentile Christians as imposing 'no greater burden'. This contrasted with the attempt to impose a yoke of ceremonies on them (v. 10). In fact, they intended to lay no burden on them at all, but only advise them on what was necessary to avoid scandal. Indeed, to be faithful to the commission of Christ (Mt. 28:19-20), it would have been quite wrong of them to have imposed any burden except the yoke and burden of Christ.

This example shows that a synod convened in the name of Christ, by the consent of several churches sharing in mutual fellowship, may declare and determine the mind of the Holy Spirit in the Scripture. They may also require that things revealed and appointed in the Scripture should be observed, because they are true and necessary. If there is evidence that the synod has the mind of the Holy Spirit and has acted with proper authority, these findings are to be received, owned and observed.

Also by Grace Publications

Pure Church
Edited By David Skull, Andrew King & Jim Sayers

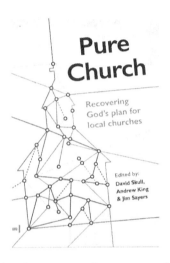

Recently there has been a growing concern for the health of gospel churches. The vision of this book is that the whole way a church should be formed, run and led should work for the health of all its members and the thriving of the church as a community of God's people. It is a church with an intentional mindset throughout, where all the dots are joined up.

The church of Christ will be completely pure only in the new creation. But local churches are to be a colony of that 'Pure Church' now. This book is a call to work towards that purity.

www.gracepublications.co.uk

Also by Grace Publications

Gospel-Driven Change
By Paul Watts

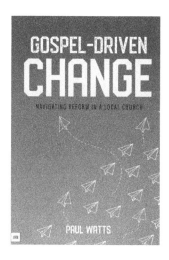

Navigating change in a church isn't easy.

However, change has to happen if the gospel is to run freely and effectively in an ever-changing culture. Written with thirty years of pastoral experience this book makes the case that only gospel-driven change is authentic, and, for the gospel's sake, it must be navigated carefully.

www.gracepublications.co.uk